SUGAR FREE...

THAT'S ME

SUGAR FREE...

THAT'S ME

by Judith Soley Majors

Cover design and illustrations
by Charles B. Wells

BALLANTINE BOOKS ● NEW YORK

To JACK, CARRIE, MOM and DAD
for their love, continual encouragement and support

Library of Congress Catalog Card Number:
78-74029

ISBN 0-345-28708-8

This edition published by arrangement with
Apple Press

Manufactured in the United States of America

First Ballantine Books Edition: April 1980

1 2 3 4 5 6 7 8 9

**American
Diabetes
Association, Inc**

OREGON AFFILIATE, INC.

S.W. Corbett
Portland, Oregon 97201
(503) 228-0849

With the blessing and the approval
of the
Dietetic Committee
American Diabetes Association, Inc.
Oregon Affiliate, Inc.

Rita Dewart

Rita Dewart
Executive Director

Moving Forward:

    Some people eat to live; I live to eat and decided diabetes was not going to rob me of one of life's pleasures! Armed with the exchange list and files of favorite recipes, and many shared by friends, I set out to substitute legal foods, in legal amounts, to be most appetizing and enjoyable.

    Along the way there have been some failures (some so bad the dog even declined to partake), many successes, many of which are shared in this book. The dishes are good, not diet-like, and will be enjoyed by anyone you serve. It is a diet for one, but food for all, and I am sure will be enjoyed by not only diabetics, their families and friends, but also any individual who wants to eat well and stay healthy!

JUDY MAJORS

With much heartfelt thanks:
OREGON DIABETES ASSOCIATION, INC., professional assistance
My family and friends, recipe testing and encouragement
T.E. Morris Jr., MD, personal counseling and advice
Willie Mae Hart, LPN, care and guidance
Marilyn Pickles, RD, teaching and training
Tim and Nancy Deggendorfer, manuscript preparation
Rita Dewart, invaluable help

4

BASIC EXCHANGE LIST

EXCHANGE PROGRAM

The exchange program offers a variety of food to fit each individual's likes and needs in specific amounts. By using the six exchange lists and foods in specified numbers and amounts to fit your diet, you can create a variety of taste sensations and almost forget you're on a diet!

The exchange program is simply a trade of one food for another in a specific food group for a food that is nearly equal in calories, carbohydrates, protein and fat. Also foods in each exchange group have similar mineral and vitamin content.

A well-balanced diet consists of foods from each food group, as no single exchange group can supply all the nutrients our body requires for good health.

The energy value of food is expressed by the calorie count. The primary energy sources are fats, proteins and carbohydrates. Sugars and starches are the most common carbohydrates. The foods in the following exchange lists work together to provide the necessary nutrients that are essential to body function.

The real trick is to carefully measure the amounts of food used. All amounts are given in household measurement.

Weights:	1 ounce or 30 grams
Volumes:	1 teaspoon or 5 milliliters
	1 tablespoon or 15 milliliters
	1 ounce or 30 milliliters
	1 cup = 8 ounces or .24 liters or 240 milliliters

FREE EXCHANGES

These foods and seasonings contain negligible amounts of protein, fat or carbohydrate and may be used in unlimited amounts:

Diet type (calorie free) beverages
Coffee
Tea
Horseradish
Unsweetened pickles (try our prize-
    winning dill pickles)
Raw lettuce
Unsweetened gelatin
Salt and pepper
Garlic
Celery salt
Radishes
Lemon juice
Lime juice

Paprika
Parsley
Mustard
Onion powder and salt
Vinegar
Cinnamon and nutmeg
Fat free bouillon
Fat free consomme
Unsweetened cranberries
Mint
Herbs
Soy sauce
Non-calorie sweeteners

LIST 1: MILK EXCHANGES
Non-Fat, Low Fat and Whole Milk

Each milk exchange contains 12 grams of carbohydrate, 8 grams of protein, a negligible amount of fat and 80 calories.

NON-FAT FORTIFIED MILK
Skim or non-fat milk	1 cup
Powdered non-fat milk (dry)	⅓ cup
Canned evaporated skim milk	½ cup
Skim type buttermilk	1 cup
Unflavored yogurt (from skim milk)	1 cup

LOW FAT FORTIFIED MILK
1% fat fortified milk (omit ½ fat exchange)	1 cup
2% fat fortified milk (omit 1 fat exchange)	1 cup
Unflavored yogurt from 2% fortified milk (omit 1 fat exchange)	1 cup

WHOLE MILK (omit 2 fat exchanges for each)
Whole milk	1 cup
Evaporated canned whole milk	½ cup
Buttermilk made from whole milk	1 cup

| Unflavored yogurt (made from whole milk) | 1 cup |
| Ice milk | 1 cup |

Milk is the leading source of calcium. It also contains protein, phosphorus, B-vitamins, magnesium and vitamins A and D. The milk exchange may be used to drink or included in recipes or added to cereal, coffee or other foods as desired. Remember to count the amount of milk added to other foods.

LIST 2:   VEGETABLE EXCHANGES

Each vegetable exchange contains approximately 5 grams of carbohydrate, 2 grams of protein and 25 calories.
*One exchange equals ½ cup unless noted.

Artichoke (1)	Chilies	Onions
Asparagus	Collards	Rhubarb
Bean Sprouts	Cucumber	Rutabagas
Beets	Dandelion	Sauerkraut
Broccoli	Egg Plant	Spinach
Brussel Sprouts	Green Beans (string)	Squash (summer)
Cabbage	Green Pepper	Tomatoes
Carrots	Kale	Tomato Juice
Cauliflower	Mushrooms	Turnips

Celery	Mustard Greens	V-8 Juice
Chard	Okra	Zucchini

The following vegetables may be used <u>raw</u> as desired, calories negligible.

Alfalfa Sprouts	Lettuce
Chicory	Onion Tops (green)
Chinese Cabbage	Parsley
Chives	Radishes
Endive	Watercress
Escarole	

*Check the bread exchange list for starchy vegetables.
Vegetables are rich sources of vitamins, and fiber is present in all vegetables.

LIST 3:   FRUIT EXCHANGES

Each fruit exchange contains 10 grams of carbohydrate and 40 calories.

Fruits may be used fresh, dried, cooked, frozen, canned or raw as long as there are no sugars added.

Fruit	Amount
Apple	1 small
Apple Juice	⅓ cup
Applesauce (sugar free)	½ cup
Apricots (fresh or dried)	2 (4 halves)
Banana	½ small
Berries:	
Blackberries	½ cup
Blueberries	½ cup
Cranberries (sugar free)	Free exchange
Raspberries	½ cup
Strawberries	¾ cup
Cantaloupe	¼ small
Cherries	10 large
Cider	⅓ cup
Dates	2
Figs	1
Grapefruit	½
Grapefruit Juice	½ cup
Grape Juice	¼ cup
Grapes	12 large
Honeydew Melon	⅛ medium
Mango	½ small
Nectarine	1 small

Fruit	Amount
Orange	1 small
Orange Juice	½ cup
Papaya	¾ cup
Peach	1 medium
Pear	1 small
Pineapple	½ cup
Pineapple Juice	⅓ cup
Plums	2 medium
Pomegranate	1 small
Prune Juice	¼ cup
Prunes	2 medium
Raisins	2 tablespoons
Tangelo	1 small
Tangerine	1 medium

Fruits supply fiber, various amounts of vitamins A and C, folacin and potassium.

LIST 4:   BREAD EXCHANGES
Breads, Cereals, Crackers and Starchy Vegetables

Each bread exchange contains 15 grams of carbohydrate, 2 grams of protein and 70 calories.

Breads	Amount
Bagel	½ small
Pumpernickel	1 slice
Rye	1 slice
Raisin	1 slice
White (including French)	1 slice
Whole Wheat	1 slice
Popover	1
English Muffin	½ small
Plain roll (bread type)	1
Hot dog bun	½
Hamburger bun	½
Croutons	½ cup plain
Dried bread crumbs	3 tablespoons
Bread sticks	4, 9″ long
Tortilla	1, 6″ diameter

Cereals	Amount
All Bran	½ cup
Bran Flakes	½ cup
Other ready to eat unsweetened cereal	¾ cup
Puffed cereal (unsweetened)	1 cup
Cereal, cooked	½ cup

13

Cereals	Amount
Grits, cooked	½ cup
Rice, cooked	½ cup
Barley, cooked	½ cup
Pasta, cooked (noodle products)	½ cup
Popcorn (popped without fat)	3 cups
Cornmeal	2 tablespoons
Flour	2½ tablespoons
Wheat germ	¼ cup
Cornstarch	2 tablespoons

Crackers	Amount
Arrowroot	3
Graham	2, 2½″ square
Oyster	20
Pretzels	25, 3½″ long × ⅛″ dia.
Rye Krisp	3
Saltines	6
Soda Crackers	4

Starchy Vegetables	Amount
Beans (dried and cooked)	½ cup
Peas (dried and cooked)	½ cup

Starchy Vegetables	Amount
Lentils (dried and cooked)	½ cup
Peas (green canned or frozen)	½ cup
Corn (canned or frozen)	⅓ cup
Corn on the cob	1 small
Lima beans	½ cup
Parsnips	⅔ cup
Potato (white)	1 small
Potato (mashed)	½ cup
Potato (sweet)	¼ cup
Pumpkin	¾ cup
Squash (winter)	½ cup
Yam	¼ cup

Miscellaneous Foods	Amount
Ice Cream (omit 2 fat exchanges)	½ cup
French Fries (omit 1 fat exchange)	8, 3″ × ½″
Potato Chips (omit 2 fat exchanges)	15
Corn Chips (omit 2 fat exchanges)	15

*Starchy vegetables are included in the bread exchange list as they contain the same amount of protein and carbohydrate as one slice of bread.

LIST 5:   MEAT EXCHANGES

Meat is divided into three categories. Each LOW FAT LEAN MEAT EXCHANGE contains 7 grams of protein, 3 grams of fat and 55 calories. For each MEDIUM FAT MEAT EXCHANGE count 75 calories and omit ½ fat exchange. For each HIGH FAT MEAT EXCHANGE count 100 calories and omit 1 fat exchange.

	Low Fat Lean Meat Exchanges (Fat Removed)	Amount
Beef:	Baby beef, chopped beef, chuck, flank steak, london broil, tenderloin plate, ribs, top and bottom round (steak and roast), all cuts rump, sirloin and tripe	1 ounce
Lamb:	Leg, rib, loin, shoulder and shank	1 ounce
Pork:	Leg, rump, center shank, smoked ham (center slices)	1 ounce
Veal:	Leg, loin, rib, cutlets	1 ounce
Poultry:	Flesh only (skin removed), chicken, turkey, cornish game hen, pheasant	1 ounce
Seafoods and Shellfish:	Any fresh or frozen fish	1 ounce

	Canned salmon, tuna, mackerel, crab or	
	lobster	¼ cup
	Clams, oysters, scallops, shrimp	1 ounce or 5 medium
	Sardines, drained	3
Cheese:	Those containing less than 5% butterfat	1 ounce
Cottage		
Cheese:	Dry, 2% butterfat	¼ cup

*Check pre-basted and liquid cured meats and poultry for sugar and fat contents.

	Medium Fat Meat Exchanges	Amount
Beef:	Ground (15% fat), corned beef (canned), rib eye, ground round	1 ounce
Pork:	Loin (all cuts), shoulder (picnic), Boston butt, broiled ham, canadian bacon	1 ounce
All:	Liver, heart, kidney, sweetbreads	1 ounce
Cheese:	Mozzarella, Ricotta, Farmer's Cheese, Parmesan, grated	1 ounce / 3 tablespoons
Eggs:	Raw or cooked (no fat added)	1

High Fat Meat Exchanges		Amount
Beef:	Ground beef (more than 20% fat), corned beef brisket, brisket, commercial hamburger, chuck, rib roasts and steaks	1 ounce
Veal:	Breast	1 ounce
Lamb:	Breast	1 ounce
Pork:	Spare ribs, loin, ground pork, sausage, country style ham, deviled ham	1 ounce
Poultry:	Duck, goose	1 ounce
Cheese:	Cheddar	1 ounce
Prepared Meats:	Hot dogs (frankfurters, wieners)	1 small
	Cold cuts (4½" × ⅛" slice)	1

LIST 6: FAT EXCHANGES

Each fat exchange contains 5 grams of fat and 45 calories.

Saturated Fats	Amount
Margarine (regular)	1 teaspoon
Butter	1 teaspoon
Bacon grease	1 teaspoon

18

Saturated Fats	Amount
Bacon, cooked crisp	1 slice
Cream, light	2 tablespoons
Cream, sour	2 tablespoons
Cream, heavy	1 tablespoon
Cream cheese	1 tablespoon
Mayonnaise	1 teaspoon
Salad dressing (mayonnaise type)	2 teaspoons
Lard	1 teaspoon

Polyunsaturated Fats	
Soft margarine (tub or stick)	1 teaspoon
Avocado	⅛, 4″ diameter
Corn Oil	1 teaspoon
Cottonseed Oil	1 teaspoon
Safflower Oil	1 teaspoon
Soy Oil	1 teaspoon
Sunflower Oil	1 teaspoon
Olive Oil	1 teaspoon
Peanut Oil	1 teaspoon
Olives	5 small
Nuts:	
Almonds	10 whole
Pecans	2 large
Spanish Peanuts	20 whole

Virginia Peanuts	10 whole
Walnuts	6 small
Other Nuts	6 small

Fats are concentrated calorie sources and should be measured carefully. The origin of fats is either animal or vegetable and they range from solid hard fats to liquid oils. Generally, vegetable fats (corn oil, peanut oil, etc.) remain liquid at room temperature. Saturated fat is often hard at room temperature and is primarily from animal food products (butter, bacon, meat fat, etc.).

APPETIZERS and BEVERAGES

HOT CRAB/SHRIMP DIP

32 Servings
1 Tablespoon = 60 Calories
½ Med Fat Meat Exchange
½ Fat Exchange

1 (8 ounce) package cream cheese, softened
1 cup crab meat or shrimp or a combination
2 tablespoons chopped sweet onion
2 tablespoons milk
½ teaspoon horseradish
½ teaspoon salt
½ teaspoon pepper
¼ teaspoon dry mustard

Mix all ingredients until well blended. Bake in small casserole dish 10-15 minutes at 350°.

Serve with celery sticks, french bread cubes or crackers.

CRAB CHEESE BITES

36 Appetizers
1 Appetizer = 65 Calories
¼ Low Fat Meat Exchange
½ Fat Exchange
⅓ Bread Exchange

8 ounces crab meat, flaked
1 teaspoon sliced green onion
4 ounces shredded swiss cheese (1 cup)
¼ cup mayonnaise
1 teaspoon lemon juice
¼ teaspoon curry powder
⅛ teaspoon pepper
1 package flaky refrigerator rolls (12 rolls)

Combine first seven ingredients and mix well. Separate each roll into 3 layers. Place on ungreased cookie sheet. Spoon on crab mixture. Bake in 400° oven for 10 to 12 minutes or until golden brown.

SAUCY CHEESE SPREAD

16 Servings
1 Tablespoon = 45 Calories
1 Fat Exchange

1 (8 ounce) package cream cheese, room temperature
¼ cup soy sauce
1 teaspoon toasted sesame seeds (optional)

   Put cheese on plate. Make holes with a fork along top. Pour soy sauce over slowly, sprinkle with sesame seeds if desired.
   Serve with crackers or vegetable sticks.

SHRIMP COCKTAIL

Serves 1 = 110 Calories
2 Low Fat Meat Exchanges

2 ounces cleaned salad shrimp
Cocktail sauce
Lemon wedge

Top cleaned salad shrimp with cocktail sauce as desired and garnish with lemon wedge. The whole family will feel special when served a shrimp cocktail.

DILLY DIP

8 Servings
1 Tablespoon = 15 Calories
¼ Low Fat Meat Exchange

½ cup mock sour cream
1 teaspoon dill weed
Dash salt and pepper

Mix all ingredients; refrigerate 4 hours to blend flavors. Use as a dip for raw vegetables or put a dollop on hot cooked green beans.

ONION DIP

6 Servings
1 Tablespoon = 20 Calories
¼ Low Fat Meat Exchange
If more than 3 tablespoons
of dip are used, ¼
bread exchange must be
added.

¾ cup mock sour cream
1 package onion Cup-of-Soup mix

Mix together and chill 4 hours before serving. Excellent as a dip for raw vegetables or tortilla strips. Also use as a vegetable or potato topping.

TOMATO MOCK COCKTAIL

Serves 4
½ Cup = 25 Calories
1 Vegetable Exchange

2 cups tomato juice
2 tablespoons lemon juice
Dash celery salt
½ teaspoon Worcestershire sauce
Drop of Tabasco (if desired)
4 lemon slices

Combine first five ingredients. Chill. Rub lemon slice around rim of glass before filling. Fill, float a lemon slice in each serving. Good served over ice cubes.

It's party perfect if you dip the edge of the glass in cocktail salt after rubbing with the lemon but before filling. You'll forget it's a "mock" cocktail.

SUNSHINE PUNCH

12 Servings (½ cup each)
1 serving = 40 Calories
1 Fruit Exchange

3 cups orange juice (unsweetened)
1 (12 ounce) can unsweetened pineapple juice
½ cup lemon juice
Artificial sweetener equal to ½ cup sugar
16 ounce bottle sugar free lemon-lime or ginger ale

Combine all ingredients except soda. Chill. Add pop just before serving. This is really attractive if served with ice molded in a jello mold or block with orange slices.

PINEAPPLE SWIRL

Serves 2
1 serving = 40 Calories
1 Fruit Exchange

1 (8 ounce) can unsweetened pineapple
2 tablespoons lime juice
½ teaspoon rum flavoring
4 ice cubes

Combine all ingredients in blender on high speed until pineapple is finely crushed and ice nearly disappears. Rub glasses with lime slice around rim and garnish with lime.

ROOT BEER FLOAT

Serves 1 = 160 Calories
1 Bread Exchange
2 Fat Exchanges

1 (8-12 ounce) sugar free root beer
½ cup vanilla ice cream

Add ice cream to chilled root beer and enjoy your treat! Ice cream should only be exchanged in diet twice weekly.

ICE CREAM FROST

Serves 1 = 160 calories
1 Bread Exchange
2 Fat Exchanges

1 (8-12 ounce) fruit flavored sugar free soda
½ cup vanilla ice cream

Blend ice cream and soda to mix. The smaller the amount of soda, the thicker the frost.

SLUSHY

Serves 1
Free Exchange

Resembles commercial "Slurpy" type drinks.

1 can sugar free soda in your choice of flavor
8 ice cubes

Put in blender until ice is finely chopped but not liquified. Children love it and it is particularly nice when you need a treat and all exchanges for the day are gone or to get between meals.

HOT CHOCOLATE

4 Servings
1 Serving = 80 Calories
1 Skim Milk Exchange

3 tablespoons cocoa
Artificial sweetener equal to 1 tablespoon sugar
3 cups skim milk

Place cocoa, sweetener, and milk in saucepan. Using a wire whip, stir constantly while heating to blend in cocoa and keep from sticking. Don't boil.

MOCK TOM AND JERRY

1 cup = 80 Calories

1 cup skim milk
Artificial sweetener to taste
Rum or brandy extract to taste
Dash of cinnamon or nutmeg

Heat skim milk slowly, stirring constantly to avoid scorching. Add flavoring according to taste. Sprinkle with your favorite spice.

BERRY MILKSHAKE

Serves 2
1 Serving = 100 Calories
1 Milk Exchange
½ Fruit Exchange

⅔ cup non-fat dry milk
1 cup raspberries (washed and drained)
½ teaspoon vanilla
8 ounces sugar free raspberry soda
2 ice cubes

     Mix all ingredients in blender. Surprisingly thick and creamy like an "ice cream" shake.

TOMATO TUMMY WARMER

Serves 4
½ Cup = 25 Calories
1 Vegetable Exchange

2 cups tomato juice
2 tablespoons lemon juice
⅛ teaspoon celery salt
1 teaspoon Worcestershire sauce
¼ teaspoon pepper

Heat first 4 ingredients. Pour into mugs and sprinkle with pepper if desired. This is good as an appetizer or late-evening snack.

EGGS, BREADS and MUFFINS

OMELETTE

1 Basic Omelette = 175 Calories
½ Fat Exchange
2 Med Fat Meat Exchanges

Basic Omelette:

2 eggs
¼ teaspoon salt
Dash pepper
1 tablespoon skim milk
½ teaspoon butter

Beat all ingredients except butter until light and frothy. Melt butter in skillet over medium heat, add the egg mixture, and as it cooks make fast circular motions around the pan to raise the layers. Shake the pan to and fro until the eggs set and spread evenly on the bottom. The motion keeps the batter running underneath to set. Fold over in half and serve. (Add filling, if any, before folding.)

I generally add filling and make 2 servings.

Omelettes are excellent quick, nourishing entrees for any meal. At lunch I often have one with a tossed salad and at dinner with a vegetable, fruit cup and muffin.

OMELETTE VARIATIONS

Denver Omelette:

    1 Basic Omelette Recipe
    ¼ cup cooked diced ham
    1 tablespoon diced green pepper
    1 teaspoon onion

Whole Omelette	2 Servings = Per Serving
1 Low Fat Meat Exchange	½ Low Fat Meat Exchange
2 Med Fat Meat Exchanges	1 Med Fat Meat Exchange
½ Fat Exchange	¼ Fat Exchange
Vegetable Negligible	Vegetable Negligible
230 calories	115 Calories

Cheese Omelette:

    1 Basic Omelette Recipe
    ¼ cup grated cheddar or 1 slice American cheese

Whole Omelette	2 Servings = Per Serving
1 High Fat Meat Exchange	½ High Fat Meat Exchange
2 Med Fat Meat Exchanges	1 Med Fat Meat Exchange
½ Fat Exchange	¼ Fat Exchange
275 calories	138 calories

<u>Seafood/Cheese Omelette:</u>

    1 Basic Omelette Recipe
    ¼ cup crab, shrimp or combination
    ¼ cup grated cheddar or 1 slice American cheese

<u>Whole Omelette</u>	<u>2 Servings = Per Serving</u>
1 Low Fat Meat Exchange	½ Low Fat Meat Exchange
1 High Fat Meat Exchange	½ High Fat Meat Exchange
2 Med Fat Meat Exchanges	1 Med Fat Meat Exchange
½ Fat Exchange	¼ Fat Exchange
330 calories	165 calories

<u>Ham and Cheese Omelette:</u>

    1 Basic Omelette Recipe
    ¼ cup chopped ham
    ¼ cup grated cheddar or 1 slice American cheese

<u>Whole Omelette</u>	<u>2 Servings = Per Serving</u>
1 Low Fat Meat Exchange	½ Low Fat Meat Exchange
1 High Fat Meat Exchange	½ High Fat Meat Exchange
2 Med Fat Meat Exchanges	1 Med Fat Meat Exchange
½ Fat Exchange	¼ Fat Exchange
330 calories	165 calories

Ham Omelette:

    1 Basic Omelette Recipe
    ¼ cup cooked diced ham

Whole Omelette	2 Servings = Per Serving
1 Low Fat Meat Exchange	½ Low Fat Meat Exchange
2 Med Fat Meat Exchanges	1 Med Fat Meat Exchange
½ Fat Exchange	¼ Fat Exchange
230 calories	115 calories

Asparagus/Cheese Omelette:

    1 Basic Omelette Recipe
    4 asparagus spears
    ¼ cup grated cheddar or 1 slice American cheese

Whole Omelette	2 Servings = Per Serving
1 High Fat Meat Exchange	½ High Fat Meat Exchange
2 Med Fat Meat Exchanges	1 Med Fat Meat Exchange
½ Fat Exchange	¼ Fat Exchange
1 Vegetable Exchange	½ Vegetable Exchange
300 calories	150 calories

WESTERN EGG

Serves 2
1 Serving = 175 Calories
2 Med Fat Meat Exchanges
½ Fat Exchange
Vegetable Negligible

1 teaspoon butter or margarine
½ teaspoon chopped onion
½ cup diced cooked ham
2 teaspoons chopped green pepper (optional)
2 eggs

Melt butter in frying pan over medium heat. Stir in onion, ham, and green pepper and cook until tender, but not brown. Add well beaten eggs. Stir gently to mix. Cook until set, turning once.

WESTERN EGG SANDWICH

1 Sandwich = 315 Calories
2 Med Fat Meat Exchanges
½ Fat Exchange
2 Bread Exchanges
Vegetable Negligible

Make Western Egg Recipe and place between two slices of bread or toast. Makes a warm sandwich. Great for brunch.

OVEN "FRIED" BACON

1 Slice = 45 Calories
1 Fat Exchange

Place bacon on broiler rack in center of 350° oven and bake 12-15 minutes. Remove and drain on paper towels. This can be stored in the refrigerator until needed and just reheat or chop and stir in vegetables or eggs as needed. Most fat will drip out during cooking.

MOCK FRIED EGGS

Serves 2
1 Serving = 87 Calories
1 Med Fat Meat Exchange
¼ Fat Exchange

½ teaspoon butter or bacon fat
2 eggs

Heat fat to cover skillet. Add eggs. Immediately add ½ teaspoon water for each egg. Cover lightly and cook to desired firmness. Season with salt and pepper to taste.

Tasty, and lower in calories than eggs fried in fat.

Eggs cooked covered are foolproof; they have the appearance of an egg over easy without turning.

DEVILED EGGS

8 Halves
2 Halves = 120 Calories
1 Med Fat Meat Exchange
1 Fat Exchange

4 hard-cooked eggs
4 teaspoons mayonnaise
½-1 teaspoon prepared mustard (to taste)
Salt and pepper (to taste)
Paprika to garnish

Peel and cut each egg in half lengthwise and remove the yolk. Mash yolks and mix with mayonnaise and seasoning. Refill the whites and sprinkle lightly with paprika.

BLUEBERRY MUFFINS

Serves 12
1 Serving = 95 Calories
1 Bread Exchange
½ Fat Exchange
Fruit Negligible

2 cups flour
2½ teaspoons baking powder
1 teaspoon salt
1 egg
1 cup skim milk
2 tablespoons melted butter or margarine
½ cup blueberries, rinsed and drained

Mix dry ingredients. Add slightly beaten egg, milk and melted butter. Mix well, but do not beat. Stir in blueberries. Spoon evenly into 12 muffin tins lined with cupcake papers. Bake at 375°, 20 to 25 minutes. Yummy warm!

CORN MUFFINS

12 Muffins
1 Muffin = 95 Calories
1 Bread Exchange
½ Fat Exchange

½ cup corn meal
1 cup flour
1 tablespoon baking powder
½ teaspoon salt
1 egg
¾ cup milk
1 tablespoon melted butter or margarine

Mix dry ingredients. Add lightly beaten egg, milk and melted butter. Bake in muffin tins lined with cupcake papers for 20 minutes at 400°.

*Be careful not to overbeat these (or any muffins) or they will have air tunnels and pointed tops.

POPOVERS

8 Servings
1 Serving = 70 Calories
1 Bread Exchange

1 cup sifted flour
½ teaspoon salt
2 eggs
1 cup skim milk

Beat all ingredients until smooth. Don't overbeat as overbeating will reduce volume. Pour into well greased muffin tins (fill ¾ full) or custard cups (fill ½ full). Bake at 425° for 40-50 minutes. Serve hot with butter.

Popovers are a unique company bread as the tops pop and they are light, crusty shells.

Popovers are delicious when filled with any creamed vegetable, seafood or meat as a main dish. Can be used for the bread exchange.

DUMPLINGS

4 Servings
1 Serving = 55 Calories
¾ Bread Exchange
Milk Negligible

½ cup flour (sifted)
1 teaspoon baking powder
¼ teaspoon salt
¼ cup skim milk

Mix dry ingredients and stir in milk until mixture is smooth. Drop into boiling liquid and boil for 5 minutes covered.

Divide number of dumplings by 4 for one serving. (I usually end up with 8 dumplings.)

Super with stewed chicken or beef stew. Also adds body to clear soups.

CHEESE CHIPS

Makes 16 chips
4 Chips = 68 Calories
¼ Bread Exchange
½ High Fat Meat Exchange

1 slice white bread (torn in small pieces)
2 ounces sharp cheddar cheese, diced

    Crumb bread and cheese in blender. With hands press crumbs together and form 16 little balls. Place on cookie sheet and flatten balls with bottom of a glass. Bake at 400° about 4 minutes on each side so chips will be crisp on both sides. Good as an appetizer, or to munch, or with a salad.

FRENCH TOAST

Serves 1 = 150 Calories
1 Bread Exchange
1 Med Fat Meat Exchange
Milk Negligible

1 egg
1 tablespoon skim milk
Drop vanilla
1 slice bread

Beat egg, skim milk, and vanilla in shallow bowl; dip bread in egg mixture, turning to coat and absorb egg mixture. Cook on a non-stick skillet or frying pan, turning once to brown both sides.

WAFFLES

Serves 4
1 Serving = 115 Calories
1 Bread Exchange
1 Fat Exchange

½ cup flour
1½ teaspoons baking powder
¼ teaspoon salt
½ cup milk
1 egg
1½ teaspoons melted butter

    Mix dry ingredients, add milk, slightly beaten egg and melted butter. Beat with wire whip until smooth. Bake in hot waffle iron. Serve with sugarless syrup or jam.

GERMAN PANCAKE

Serves 2
1 Serving = 270 Calories
¼ Milk Exchange
1½ Bread Exchanges
1 Med Fat Meat Exchange
1½ Fat Exchanges

½ cup skim milk
½ cup flour
2 eggs
1 tablespoon melted butter
Little salt, cinnamon or nutmeg (3 shakes)

Beat together by hand first three ingredients. Melt butter in ovenproof frying pan. Pour all ingredients into frying pan. Sprinkle with spice. Bake at 425°-450° for 12 minutes, until brown and puffy.

BUTTERMILK PANCAKES

Makes 10, 2-3 Inch Pancakes
2 Pancakes = 70 Calories
1 Bread Exchange

1 egg
1¼ cup buttermilk
2 tablespoons oil
1 cup flour (unsifted)
½ teaspoon baking soda
½ teaspoon salt
1 teaspoon baking powder

Mix all ingredients well with mixer or wire whip until smooth. Cook on hot teflon griddle until bubbles form on one side. Turn and brown on other side.

Enjoy with your own fruit jam or syrup.

SOUPS and SANDWICHES

VEGETABLE SOUP

Makes 3 Quarts
1 Cup = 45 Calories
1 Vegetable Exchange
¼ Bread Exchange

1 large marrow soup bone
3 quarts water

Cover bone with three quarts cold water and bring to boil. Lower heat and simmer half hour. Skim top of pot. Refrigerate broth and remove fat off the top. Reheat stock (with bone) and add:

½ teaspoon pepper
1 quart canned tomatoes
1 bay leaf
½ cup celery
1 small package frozen mixed vegetables
1 potato diced
¼ cup chopped cabbage
1 tablespoon salt
½ cup egg noodles (uncooked)
1 large chopped onion

You may also add any chopped vegetable of your choice or drain any leftovers in your refrigerator and add them. Bring to boil. Simmer four hours, season with additional salt and pepper.

54

QUICK POTATO SOUP

4 Servings
1 Cup = 110 Calories
1 Bread Exchange
½ Milk Exchange

2 cups diced peeled potatoes
2 cups water
⅓ cup chopped onion
½ package frozen chopped broccoli
2 beef bouillon cubes
1 teaspoon salt
¼ teaspoon pepper
1 teaspoon Worchestershire sauce or 1 tablespoon chopped pimento
1½ cups skim milk

Combine all ingredients except milk. Bring to a boil and simmer 15 minutes. Add milk and heat through.

CLAM CHOWDER

Serves 2
1 Serving = 270 Calories
1 Fat Exchange
½ Bread Exchange
1 Milk Exchange
2 Low Fat Meat Exchanges

1 strip bacon, diced
½ small onion, chopped
1 small potato, diced
4 ounces canned clams
2 cups milk
Salt and pepper
Dash paprika to garnish

Cook bacon over medium heat in saucepan. Add onion, potato and clams with their liquid. Simmer about 15 minutes or until vegetables are tender. Add milk and seasonings. Garnish with paprika.

*If your diet can handle an additional ¼ fat exchange (12 calories), add ¼ teaspoon butter to top of each cup before sprinkling on paprika.

OYSTER STEW

Serves 6
1 Serving = 173 Calories
2 Low Fat Meat Exchanges
½ Milk Exchange
½ Fat Exchange

1 pint fresh oysters
3 cups skim milk
1 teaspoon salt
¼ teaspoon pepper
1 tablespoon Worchestershire sauce (optional for zip)
1 tablespoon butter
Paprika for garnish

Cook oysters in their liquid about 3 minutes on medium heat (edges will curl).
Add milk and heat to the boiling point, taking care not to boil. Add seasonings. Drop ½
teaspoon butter on top of each serving and sprinkle lightly with paprika.

MOM'S SPECIAL
(My Favorite Sandwich)

Serves 1
1 Serving = 215 Calories
1 High Fat Meat Exchange
1 Bread Exchange
1 Fat Exchange

1 strip bacon cut in half
½ english muffin
1 slice cheddar cheese
1 slice tomato (large or 2 small)

Partially cook bacon and pat with paper towel. Place muffin on broiler rack and top with cheese, tomato and the bacon in order given. Broil about 4 inches from heat until bacon crisps and cheese is melted and bubbly.

*Good on pumpernickel bread for a change of pace. I even like this for breakfast.

GRILLED CRAB AND CHEESE SANDWICHES

2 Servings
1 Serving = 380 Calories
2 Low Fat Meat Exchanges
1½ Fat Exchanges
¾ High Fat Meat Exchange
2 Bread Exchanges

4 ounces crab meat
2 teaspoons mayonnaise
Dash salt and pepper
4 slices sandwich bread
2 slices processed cheese (¾ ounce)
1 teaspoon soft butter

Mix crab and mayonnaise. Add salt and pepper. Top one slice bread with half crab mixture and a slice of cheese. Put on top slice of bread. Spread outside sparingly with butter and grill until lightly brown on both sides and cheese is melted.

Serve with fresh fruit cup.

OPEN FACE SOUR DOUGH CRAB SANDWICHES

8 Sandwiches
1 Serving = 195 Calories
1 Low Fat Meat Exchange
¼ High Fat Meat Exchange
1 Fat Exchange
1 Bread Exchange

1 cup crab meat
¼ cup diced celery
2 teaspoons finely chopped onion or chives
½ cup shredded cheddar cheese (2 ounces)
8 teaspoons mayonnaise
4 sour dough english muffins

Combine crab meat, celery, onion and cheese. Add mayonnaise and blend. Spread on halved sour dough muffins. Broil until hot and browned.

If the muffins are cold, I toast them lightly under the broiler before topping with crab mixture.

ALL-AMERICAN HAMBURGERS

Serves 5
1 Serving = 290 Calories
2 Med Fat Meat Exchanges
2 Bread Exchanges

1 pound extra lean ground meat
5 hamburger buns

Divide meat into 5 equal portions. Broil to desired doneness turning once. You can also pan fry on hot ungreased salted skillet, but blot meat with a paper towel before putting on bun. Serve on warm or toasted buns. Garnish with lettuce, mustard, onion slice, dill pickles and a tomato slice piled high. You'll forget you're on a special diet!

HOT DOG!

Serves 4
1 Serving = 240 Calories
on bun
1 High Fat Meat Exchange
2 Bread Exchanges

1 Serving = 170 Calories
on bread
1 High Fat Meat Exchange
1 Bread Exchange

4 hot dogs
4 hot dog buns <u>or</u> 4 slices bread

Broil hot dogs about 3 inches from heat. Turn to avoid over browning. Cook until juice (fats) run out and hot dog is done. Place on warm bun or bread. Garnish with mustard and chopped sweet onion. Almost like roasted over a campfire!

CHEESY DOG

Serves 4
1 Serving = 290 Calories
                on bun
2 Bread Exchanges
1½ High Fat Meat Exchanges

1 Serving = 220 Calories
                on bread
1 Bread Exchange
1½ High Fat Meat Exchanges

1 Hot Dog = 150 Calories
              no bread
1½ High Fat Meat Exchanges

4 hot dogs
2 ounces grated cheese
4 hot dog buns or 4 slices bread

Split hot dogs lengthwise deep enough to insert cheese. Be careful not to cut in half. Pack cheese into slit. Bake in 325° oven until cheese is melted and outside of hot dog becomes crisp. Serve hot.

CHICKEN SALAD SANDWICH

Serves 1
1 Sandwich = 240 Calories
2 Bread Exchanges
1 Low Fat Meat Exchange
1 Fat Exchange

¼ cup cooked chopped or ground chicken
1 teaspoon chopped celery
1 teaspoon mayonnaise
Salt and pepper to taste
2 slices bread
1 lettuce leaf
1 tomato slice

Mix first four ingredients until well blended. Refrigerate. At serving time place on bread. Garnish with lettuce leaf and tomato slice. For a change of pace try chicken salad on whole wheat toast.

*This is a great way to use any lean leftover meat, just simply exchange for the chicken.

SAUCES, TOPPINGS and GRAVY

SEAFOOD COCKTAIL SAUCE

Free Exchange

¾ cup chili sauce
4 tablespoons lemon juice
1 tablespoon horseradish
1 teaspoon Worcestershire sauce
1 teaspoon finely chopped onion (if desired)
¼ teaspoon salt
Dash of pepper

Combine all ingredients and chill. Serve over crab, shrimp or oysters.
To extend the seafood I often finely chop a small amount of celery and mix in with the seafood and sauce.

TARTAR SAUCE

Makes ½ Cup
1 Tablespoon = 25 Calories
½ Fat Exchange

½ cup low calorie mayonnaise
1 tablespoon chopped dill pickle
1 teaspoon chopped onion
½ teaspoon horseradish
Salt and pepper to taste
1 teaspoon snipped parsley
Squirt of lemon juice

Combine all ingredients. Chill thoroughly to blend flavors. Excellent with fish.

*This can also be used as a sandwich spread for a change of pace.

TERIYAKI SAUCE

Free Food
Calories Negligible

1 cup soy sauce
2 cloves crushed garlic
1 teaspoon dry mustard
Artificial sweetener to equal 1 teaspoon sugar
2 teaspoons ground ginger

Combine all ingredients in a jar with tight lid. Refrigerate, and sauce will keep several weeks.

HORSERADISH SAUCE

16 Servings
1 Tablespoon = 25 Calories
½ Fat Exchange

1 cup whipped cream
1 teaspoon horseradish (more if desired)
1 teaspoon catsup
Artificial sweetener (optional)

Blend all ingredients well. Refrigerate until serving time. Delicious with ham, prime rib or your favorite beef roast. For a sweet-spicy taste add a bit of artificial (liquid) sweetener.

*Make plenty—guests usually ask for seconds.

CHEESE SAUCE

Makes 1 Cup
½ Cup = 140 Calories
¾ Bread Exchange
½ Milk Exchange
½ High Fat Meat Exchange

1 cup skim milk
2 tablespoons flour
½ teaspoon salt
¼ teaspoon pepper
¼ cup grated sharp cheddar or 1 ounce diced

Heat milk. Mix flour to a smooth paste with a little cold water, add to milk stirring constantly. When mixture thickens add seasonings and cheese and stir until cheese is melted and sauce is smooth.

Excellent over vegetables.

BLUE CHEESE TOPPING

16 Servings
1 Tablespoon = 12 Calories
¼ Fat Exchange

1 (8 ounce) carton yogurt (plain)
¼ teaspoon onion powder
½ teaspoon salt
½ teaspoon garlic powder
2 tablespoons crumbled blue cheese

Combine all ingredients and chill 2 hours to develop flavors.
This adds character to potatoes and makes green vegetables something special.

CREAM CHEESE TOPPING

8 servings
1 Tablespoon = 45 Calories
1 Fat Exchange

1 (3 ounce) package cream cheese, softened
3 tablespoons milk

Beat cheese and milk until light and fluffy.
Use on desserts and fruits.

SAUCY CHEESE TOPPING

(For Potatoes and Vegetables)

16 Servings
1 Tablespoon = 20 Calories
¼ Med Fat Meat Exchange

2 tablespoons flour
1 cup skim milk
¼ teaspoon dry mustard (optional)
½ teaspoon salt
¼ teaspoon pepper
½ cup grated American cheese

Make a paste of flour and 2 tablespoons milk in saucepan. Stirring constantly, gradually add the remaining milk. Cook until thickened. Add seasoning and cheese and stir over low heat until thickened.

HERB-CHEESE POTATO TOPPING

16 Servings
1 Tablespoon = 15 Calories
¼ Low Fat Meat Exchange

1 cup low calorie cottage cheese
2 tablespoons buttermilk
½ teaspoon dill weed
½ teaspoon tarragon
½ teaspoon salt
½ teaspoon pepper
Dash garlic powder

Combine and mix thoroughly. Chill. Keep refrigerated.

*This is also yummy to dip raw vegetables in.

WHITE SAUCE

Makes 1 Cup
½ Cup = 90 Calories
¾ Bread Exchange
½ Milk Exchange

1 cup skim milk
2 tablespoons flour
½ teaspoon salt
¼ teaspoon pepper
½ teaspoon onion powder (optional)

Heat milk. Mix flour to a smooth paste with a little cold water. Add. Stir constantly over medium heat until thickened. Add seasonings.

This makes an excellent base for creamed tuna, turkey, etc. Just remember to add your meat exchanges and calories.

JELLIED CRANBERRY SAUCE

Serves 10-12
Free Food

4 cups fresh cranberries
1½ cups water
Artificial sweetener equal to ¾ cup sugar
1 envelope unflavored gelatin dissolved in ¼ cup cold water

In large saucepan combine cranberries and all of water. Bring to a boil, turn down heat and simmer 10 minutes. Add sweetener. Add the cold water/gelatin mixture and stir into hot mixture until completely dissolved. Chill in large bowl or salad mold.

*Gelatin gives the artificially sweetened cranberries a bit of body; otherwise I find artificially sweetened berries get very watery.

HAM SAUCE

6 Servings
2 Tablespoons = 40 Calories
1 Fruit Exchange

1 tablespoon cornstarch
¼ teaspoon cinnamon
Dash of cloves
1½ cups water
1 tablespoon vinegar
Sugar substitute to equal ⅓ cup sugar
½ cup raisins

Mix all ingredients except raisins in saucepan. Stir constantly over low heat until mixture thickens. Remove from heat and add raisins. Let stand 15 minutes before serving.

FREE GRAVY

Free Food
Calories Negligible

Remove all fat from your meat or poultry drippings or stock. I do this by refrigerating the drippings or soup stock until the fat comes to the top, hardens and lifts right off. If I'm in a hurry I drop a tray of ice cubes in the drippings and the fat will freeze right to them. When using ice, work fast or the cubes will melt and you'll have a watery mess.

Freeze any leftover defatted drippings for later use or to dress up leftovers.

1 cup fat free drippings or stock
1 tablespoon cornstarch
2 drops Kitchen Bouquet (for brown gravy) or yellow food
   coloring for light gravy

Heat drippings or stock in saucepan. Remove about 2 tablespoons of liquid and mix cornstarch to dissolve. Return to pan, add the Kitchen Bouquet, and stir until thickened. For beef gravy I like the flavor ½ teaspoon of onion powder adds.

MUSHROOM SAUCE

Free Food
Calories Negligible

Make Free Gravy Recipe and add one small can of drained mushrooms.
Adds variety to ground meats, and leftovers become plan-overs.

MOCK SOUR CREAM

Makes 2¼ Cups
1 Tablespoon = 15 Calories
¼ Meat Exchange

1 pint low fat cottage cheese
¼ teaspoon salt
¼ cup lemon juice

In blender mix cottage cheese, salt and lemon juice until smooth. Use as sour cream.

CHOCOLATE SAUCE

Makes 1 cup
1 Tablespoon = 25 Calories
½ Fat Exchange

1 tablespoon butter
2 tablespoons cocoa
1 tablespoon cornstarch
1 cup skim milk
½ teaspoon vanilla
Artificial sweetener to equal ⅓ cup sugar

Mix all ingredients until well blended in saucepan. Cook over medium heat stirring constantly until slightly thickened. Remove from heat and set pan in ice water and stir until completely cold. Sauce thickens as it cools. (If not cooled over ice, the chocolate sauce will get a pudding-like skin and be rubbery.)

I like this over ice cream or for a fancy dessert over puff shells that have been filled with ice cream.

THIN MAPLE SYRUP

Free Food

1 can sugar free cream soda
½ teaspoon butter flavoring
½ teaspoon maple extract
Artificial sweetener to equal 2 teaspoons sugar can be added
    if desired. The soda adds much sweetener.

    Combine all ingredients and bring to a boil. Serve warm. Leftover syrup will keep refrigerated.

FRUIT JAM

> Measure as for Fruit Exchange
> Generally ½ cup = 1 Fruit Exchange = 40
> Calories

2 cups fruit
1 teaspoon lemon juice
1½ teaspoon (½ envelope) unflavored gelatin
Artificial sweetener to taste (I use ½ teaspoon liquid)

Use fresh berries, apricots, peaches, pears, pineapple or a combination. Cut up the fruit and simmer <u>without</u> water about 6 minutes. Turn heat to medium and cook until fruit is about half cooked and there is lots of liquid in the pan. Add lemon juice and gelatin which has been dissolved and is 3 tablespoons of the juice. Mix well. Add sweetener to taste. Refrigerate. Enjoy!

*Peach, pear and pineapple are a super combination.

SPAGHETTI SAUCE

Serves 4
1 Serving (¾ cup) = 250 Calories
3 Med Fat Meat Exchanges
1 Vegetable Exchange

1 pound extra lean ground beef
1 teaspoon salt
2 cups tomato sauce (sugarless)
1 cup water
1 clove crushed garlic
½ teaspoon oregano
1 tablespoon minced onion

Brown meat, pour off fat. Add remaining ingredients, bring to a boil and reduce to simmer for 2 hours.

Serve over cooked spaghetti but remember to add pasta in your daily exchanges. Pasta—½ cup = 1 bread exchange.

*If meat looks rather fat, refrigerate and lift off fat. Reheat over low heat and enjoy!

MAIN DISHES

DEVILED CRAB OR SHRIMP

4 Servings
1 Serving = 235 Calories
1 Fat Exchange
½ Bread Exchange
¼ Milk Exchange
2 Low Fat Meat Exchanges
¼ High Fat Meat Exchange

4 teaspoons butter
1 tablespoon finely chopped onion
2 tablespoons flour
1 cup skim milk
½ teaspoon Worchestershire sauce
½ teaspoon dry mustard

½ teaspoon salt
¼ teaspoon pepper
2 cups crab, salad shrimp
  or a combination
¼ cup grated cheese
¼ cup bread crumbs

Melt butter in saucepan. Add onion and cook until soft but not brown. Add flour to make a paste. Slowly add milk and stir constantly with a wire whip until smooth and thickened. Add seasonings and shellfish. Pour into individual serving dishes, scallop shells or a one quart casserole. Top with cheese and bread crumbs. Bake at 375° for 20 minutes.

QUICK SEAFOOD NEWBERG

4 Servings
1 Serving = 225 Calories
1¼ Bread Exchange
2 Low Fat Meat Exchanges
½ Fat Exchange

1 (10 ounces) can Cream of Shrimp soup
2 tablespoons sherry or 1 tablespoon sherry, 1 tablespoon milk
8 ounces shrimp, crab, lobster, scallops or a combination of
    the shellfish
4 slices toast or 4 popovers

    Heat undiluted soup in saucepan with sherry. Add shellfish. Heat until hot and bubbly. Serve on toast or in popovers.

GOLDEN BROILED HALIBUT STEAKS

Serves 6
1 Serving = 190 Calories
3 Low Fat Meat Exchanges
½ Fat Exchange

3 halibut steaks (approximately 8 ounces each)
1 tablespoon grated onion
2 tablespoons lemon juice
Dash of salt, pepper and thyme
1 tablespoon melted butter
Paprika to garnish
Lemon wedges

Place steaks on broiler pan. Combine onions, lemon juice, salt, pepper, and thyme with butter. Baste steaks with half of the butter mixture. Broil 3 inches from the heat for 5 minutes. Turn. Baste with remaining sauce and continue broiling until fish is white and flakes easily with a fork.

Garnish with paprika and lemon wedges.

SHRIMP OR CRAB AND CHEESE

4 Servings
1 Serving = 245 Calories
1 Low Fat Meat Exchange
1 High Fat Meat Exchange
½ Fat Exchange
1 Bread Exchange
Vegetable Negligible

4 ounces of crab or shrimp
2 teaspoons mayonnaise
Dash salt and pepper
2 english muffins, halved
4 slices tomato
4 slices cheddar, sharp

Mix crab or shrimp with mayonnaise; add salt and pepper. Place on muffin halves. Top with slice of tomato and slice of cheddar. Broil until hot and bubbly and muffin edges are lightly browned.

BAKED SALMON STEAK

Serves 2
1 Serving = 190 Calories
3 Low Fat Meat Exchanges
½ Fat Exchange

1 (6 ounce) salmon steak
1 tablespoon finely chopped onion
1 teaspoon butter or margarine
1 tablespoon lemon juice
Salt and pepper to taste

Place salmon steak in baking dish and top with remaining ingredients. Bake at 350° uncovered for approximately 15 minutes or until fish flakes easily with a fork.
If desired, garnish with lemon slice and fresh parsley.

BAKED HALIBUT WITH SOUR CREAM & CHEESE

Serves 4
1 Serving = 230 Calories
3 Low Fat Meat Exchanges
1 Fat Exchange
¼ Med Fat Meat Exchange

1 pound halibut fillets
¼ cup chopped green onion (tops too)
½ cup sour cream
⅛ teaspoon pepper
¼ teaspoon salt
Dash of dill weed (optional)
2 tablespoons parmesan cheese

Place halibut in baking dish. Combine all ingredients except cheese and pour over halibut. Bake in a preheated 350° oven for 20 minutes.

Sprinkle cheese on top and broil just long enough to lightly brown the cheese.

COQUILLES ST. JACQUES

Serves 6
1 Serving = 190 Calories
2 Low Fat Meat Exchanges
½ Bread Exchange
1 Fat Exchange

1 pound fresh scallops
1 cup dry sherry
½ bay leaf
½ pound fresh mushrooms
2 tablespoons butter or margarine
1 tablespoon lemon juice
2 tablespoons diced onion
½ teaspoon salt
⅛ teaspoon pepper
1½ tablespoons flour

Topping:

¼ teaspoon paprika
Dash cayenne (optional)
1 tablespoon parmesan cheese
3 tablespoons bread crumbs

Barely simmer scallops 10 minutes in sherry with bay leaf. Saute mushrooms and onions in butter. Add flour and stir in wine broth, add lemon juice. Cook, stirring until thickened. Add salt, pepper and scallops.

Mix topping ingredients together. Sprinkle over the top. Bake at 325° for 25 minutes.

QUICK BROILED SHRIMP

2 Shrimp
1 Serving = 55 Calories
1 Low Fat Meat Exchange

2 medium shrimp
Teriyaki sauce (see recipe)

Dip shrimp into teriyaki sauce. Broil 3 inches from heat until pinkish white. Turn, broil other side until pink and starting to brown. Brush with additional sauce to keep shrimp from drying out.

TERIYAKI SEAFOOD

Marinate your portion of fish or seafood one hour before broiling or cooking on the barbecue for a change of pace.

POACHED FISH

Serves 6
1 Serving = 165 Calories
3 Low Fat Meat Exchanges

3 fish fillets (fresh or frozen), 1½ pounds
2 cups water
¼ cup lemon juice
1 small onion
1 teaspoon salt
3 peppercorns or ¼ teaspoon pepper
½ bay leaf
½ cup dry white wine (if desired)
Paprika to garnish

Thaw frozen fish and remove skin and bones if necessary. Cut fish into 6 portions. Place fish in a 10-inch frying pan. Mix liquids and seasonings. Bring poaching liquid to a boil and pour over fish. Cover and simmer (careful not to boil) for 5-10 minutes or until fish flakes easily with a fork. Sprinkle with paprika. Garnish with lemon slices.

CIOPPINO

Serves 8
1 Serving = 240 Calories
3½ Low Fat Meat Exchanges
½ Fat Exchange
1 Vegetable Exchange

4 teaspoons oil
1 large onion, chopped coarsely
1 green pepper, chopped
1 clove garlic, peeled and finely chopped
16 ounces tomato juice
8 ounces tomato sauce
1 cup water
1 cup white wine
1 bay leaf

⅛ teaspoon rosemary
⅛ teaspoon thyme
⅛ teaspoon fennel
2 teaspoons salt
¼ teaspoon pepper
1 pound large shell red shrimp
1 crab, cracked and cooked
½ pound scallops
½ pound fish fillets

    In large pot, heat oil and cook onions, green pepper and garlic until tender, but not brown. Add remaining ingredients except seafood. Simmer covered 1 hour. Prepare seafood, break crab into pieces, devein shrimp (cut down back with scissors and remove veins). Remove garlic and bay leaf. Add seafood and simmer covered 20 minutes.
    This is really messy but tasty and fun to eat.

SKINNY HANGTOWN FRY

Serves 2
1 Serving = 230 Calories
1 Low Fat Meat Exchange
2 Med Fat Meat Exchanges
½ Fat Exchange
Milk Negligible

6 medium size oysters
1 teaspoon butter
4 eggs
2 tablespoons skim milk
¼ teaspoon Worchestershire sauce
Dash of salt and pepper
*May add 1 tablespoon chopped green pepper or onion

Chop oysters in ¾ inch pieces and fry in melted butter about 2 minutes. Beat remaining ingredients and pour into pan over oysters. Gently lift oyster pieces to let egg mixture flow underneath. When set on the bottom, carefully turn it over and cook about a minute or until desired dryness. Serve with lemon wedges.

QUICK FONDUE

Serves 2
1 Serving = 270 Calories
with bread
2 High Fat Meat Exchanges
1 Bread Exchange

1 Serving = 225 Calories
with vegetables
2 High Fat Meat Exchanges
1 Vegetable Exchange

¼ cup white wine
4 ounces diced swiss cheese
⅛ teaspoon garlic powder
⅛ teaspoon pepper
1 teaspoon sherry or sherry flavoring
2 slices bread (french or rye) cut in cubes or raw vegetables
   (celery, cauliflower, green pepper, etc.)

Heat wine and add cheese, stirring continually until smooth. Add seasoning and sherry. Serve hot, with bread or vegetables for dipping.

Good change-of-pace lunch or can be used as an appetizer.

SAVORY CHICKEN BREASTS

1 Serving = 230 Calories
3 Low Fat Meat Exchanges
1 Fat Exchange
½ Bread Exchange

2 fryer breasts (approximately 8 ounces each)
1 can Cream of Mushroom soup
½ cup dry white wine
½ teaspoon seasoning salt

Skin, bone and halve fryer breasts. Mix together undiluted soup, wine and salt. Pour over chicken and bake covered at 350° for 30 minutes. Uncover and cook an additional 15 minutes.

Serve with sauce over chicken. Excellent over rice or noodles. For ½ cup rice or noodles, add one bread exchange and 70 calories.

SAUCY CHICKEN WITH MUSHROOMS

Serves 4
1 Serving = 220 Calories
3 Low Fat Meat Exchanges
1 Bread Exchange
1 Serving without rice = 150 Calories
3 Low Fat Meat Exchanges
Vegetable Negligible

2 fryer breasts (approximately 8 ounces each)
1 small can mushrooms, drained (reserving liquid)
1 cube chicken bouillon
¼ cup dry white wine
1 teaspoon chopped onion or ½ teaspoon dry onion bits
¼ teaspoon curry powder
¼ teaspoon pepper

Skin and bone chicken breasts and separate lengthwise. (Often your favorite butcher will do this without charge.) Drain mushrooms. Heat mushroom juice and last 5 ingredients until cube dissolves. Add mushrooms and pour over chicken. Cook covered 30 minutes, uncover and bake an additional 15 minutes.

Serve alone with sauce or over 2 cups of cooked rice. If I am serving it over rice, I quarter the chicken halves before cooking.

CHICKEN CACCIATORE WITH POTATOES

5 Servings
1 Serving = 305 Calories
3 Low Fat Meat Exchanges
1 Vegetable Exchánge
1 Bread Exchange
1 Fat Exchange

1 fryer (2½ pounds) cut-up
1 tablespoon butter
1 green pepper, chopped or sliced
1 can mushrooms, drained
1½ cups tomato juice
1 teaspoon oregano
⅛ teaspoon chili powder
1 teaspoon salt
¼ teaspoon pepper
5 small potatoes, peeled and halved

In a large frying pan brown chicken in melted butter. Pour off fat. Add remaining ingredients except potatoes. Bring to a boil. Cover and simmer 20 minutes. Add potatoes and cook an additional 20 minutes or until chicken and potatoes are tender.

TERIYAKI CHICKEN BREASTS

Serves 4
1 Serving = 165 Calories
3 Low Fat Meat Exchanges

2 whole chicken breasts (about ½ pound each)
Teriyaki sauce (see recipe)

Cut chicken breasts in half lengthwise and bone if desired. (I always ask the butcher to bone them.) Marinate in sauce in refrigerator 2-3 hours. I often marinate all day or overnight if I am going to be gone. Oven broil or barbecue over charcoal, turning once. Baste with remaining sauce during cooking.

CHICKEN MARENGO

Serves 4
1 Serving = 210 Calories
3 Low Fat Meat Exchanges
1 Fat Exchange

2½ to 3 pounds frying chicken
Salt and pepper
4 teaspoons margarine
1 tablespoon cornstarch
½ cup dry white wine
1 clove crushed garlic
1 can (8 ounces) cut-up tomatoes
3 chopped fresh tomatoes
1 can or ½ pound fresh mushrooms

Season chicken with salt and pepper and brown in margarine. Cover and simmer about 30 minutes. Remove chicken. Mix cornstarch with wine and pour into pan with drippings. Add garlic. Stir over low heat until thickened. Add the canned tomatoes and bring to a boil. Add fresh vegetables and chicken and simmer for 15-20 minutes.

ROAST CHICKEN

1 ounce cooked or
1 Slice (3 × 2 × ⅛) = 55 Calories
1 Low Fat Meat Exchange

Rinse bird with cold water. Place chicken on rack breast side up. Season with salt and pepper. Roast at 375° approximately 25 minutes per pound.

Super for salads, sandwiches or just plain good eating!

*Defat some of the drippings and ovenbrown potatoes, during last 30 minutes while chicken finishes cooking.

STEWED CHICKEN

Serves 4
1 Serving with butter = 210 Calories
3 Low Fat Meat Exchanges
1 Fat Exchange

1 Serving without butter = 165 Calories
3 Low Fat Meat Exchanges

*if making dumplings add dumpling
calories and exchanges

1 cut-up fryer
1 can chicken broth
Salt and pepper
2 teaspoons butter (optional)

Brown chicken in salt or butter. Cover with chicken broth and season as desired. Bake at 325° tightly covered about 45 minutes. Remove from oven and make dumplings in broth. For a gravy, broth may be thickened with a cornstarch and water paste.

I use a fryer rather than a stewer as the younger chicken is more tender, has less fat and takes less time to cook.

SUPER STUFFING
POULTRY DRESSING

Makes 3½ quarts
½ Cup = 175 Calories
1 Bread Exchange
1½ Fat Exchanges
Vegetable Negligible

1 loaf of bread (1 pound)
1¼ sticks margarine (or ½ margarine and ½ butter)
1 medium onion
2 teaspoons salt
½ teaspoon pepper
1 cup chopped fresh celery leaves
½ teaspoon poultry seasoning

Remove soft inside of loaf and crumb or cube in a large bowl. Melt margarine in frying pan on medium low heat. Soak bread crusts in hot water, squeeze out dry and crumb crusts. Add finely chopped onion to melted margarine in pan and cook until light golden brown. Add soaked, crumbed crusts and brown lightly. Stir crusts often to avoid sticking. Mix the brown crumbs with the dry ones in bowl. Add other seasonings. Pack lightly in bird.

*This dressing freezes well. Always warm dressing before stuffing bird (to restrict bacteria growth). Stuff bird just before cooking time.

TURKEY TIPS

To Thaw:

Leave turkey in original bag and thaw in one of the following ways:

A) Place on tray or in a baking dish with sides (to prevent moisture from leaking in refrigerator) for approximately 4 hours per pound. Large birds take 3 to 4 days.

B) Place in grocery bag on tray at room temperature. Allow approximately 1 hour per pound to thaw.

C) Cover with cold water in original bag about ½ hour per pound.

Take special care to refrigerate or cook turkey as soon as it is thawed. Discard original wrapper.

Rinse bird well before cooking, remove neck and giblets from cavity, rinse well and pat dry. Stuff or cook as directed.

Roast at 325° until inner temperature (thermometer inserted in breast or thick part of thigh) reaches 185-190°. Do not let thermometer touch bone.

Turkey is done when thermometer reaches 185°, when thick part of leg feels soft when pinched between fingers and leg and thigh move easily.

ROASTING THE BIRD

To roast the turkey, place it breast up on a stand-up type rack in a shallow roasting pan. (The bottom half of your oven broiler pan may be perfect.) Brush it with a little butter, margarine or cooking oil unless it is self basted. Insert meat thermometer. Place an aluminum foil "tent" loosely over bird to prevent the skin from drying out. (Also helps keep your oven cleaner.) Remove foil last ½ hour or 45 minutes so bird will become golden brown.

ROASTING TIMETABLE
(325° Oven)

Bird Weight	Approximate Time
6 - 8 pounds	3 - 3½ hours
8 - 12 pounds	3½ - 4½ hours
12 - 16 pounds	4½ - 5½ hours
16 - 20 pounds	5½ - 6½ hours
20 - 24 pounds	6½ - 7 hours

When planning dinner I always allow an extra ½ hour of cooking time in case the bird is broad breasted and needs more time to reach 185°. Unstuffed birds take about ½ hour less.

MEAT LOAF

Serves 8
1 Serving = 240 Calories
3 Med Fat Meat Exchanges
¼ Vegetable Exchange

1½ pounds ground beef (extra lean)
¼ cup cracker crumbs
2 eggs
½ cup tomato juice (or V-8 juice)
¼ cup finely chopped onion
1 teaspoon salt
1 teaspoon Worchestershire sauce
1 teaspoon garlic salt

Combine all ingredients, mix well and shape into a loaf in shallow baking dish. Bake 350° for one hour. Lift meat loaf from fat juices in pan and continue cooking on a cooking rack over the pan for 10 minutes. Excellent hot or cold.

MEAT LOAF WITH BREAD CRUMBS

8 Servings
1 Serving = 250 Calories
3 Med Fat Meat Exchanges
⅓ Bread Exchange

¾ cup coarse bread crumbs
⅔ cup tomato juice (or V-8 juice)
2 pounds ground beef (extra lean)
½ cup chopped onions
1 teaspoon salt
½ teaspoon pepper
1 teaspoon Worchestershire sauce
⅛ teaspoon garlic powder

Soak the bread crumbs in the tomato juice to color. Mix remaining ingredients together. Blend well. Shape in loaf and bake at 350° for an hour and 15 minutes.

Sometimes I dribble a teaspoon of catsup across the top before baking.

MARINATED FLANK STEAK

Serves 2
1 Serving = 165 Calories
3 Low Fat Meat Exchanges

8 ounces flank steak
2 tablespoons soy sauce
¼ teaspoon garlic powder
¼ teaspoon black pepper

Score flank steak across the grain. Marinate in the refrigerator in soy sauce and spices. Broil or charcoal grill until desired doneness, turning once. Baste with any left-over marinade while cooking.

Slice cooked steak against the grain in thin strips. Excellent alone or with horseradish sauce.

POT ROAST WITH VEGETABLES
(One Pot Meal)

Serves 5
1 Serving = 440 Calories
4 Med Fat Meat Exchanges
1 Vegetable Exchange
1 Bread Exchange
1 Fat Exchange

1 (2 pound) beef chuck roast (boneless)
1 teaspoon salt
1½ cups water
5 carrots, pared
5 medium potatoes, pared
5 small onions

Trim fat, brown meat in salt over medium heat; add water, cover and bake one hour at 325°. Add vegetables and continue cooking an additional 1½ hours adding additional water if necessary. Serve with meat juices that have been skimmed and thickened with 2 teaspoons cornstarch.

PRIME STANDING RIB ROAST

1 Ounce or 1 Slice ($2 \times 3 \times \frac{1}{8}$ inches) =
55 Calories
1 Low Fat Meat Exchange
(Lean Only)

4-8 pound rib roast (2 or 3 bones)
1 teaspoon salt
$\frac{1}{8}$ teaspoon pepper
$\frac{1}{2}$ teaspoon garlic powder or onion powder

You can have butcher loosen the bones to make carving easier.

Season meat and place in open baking pan, fat side up. Bake ten minutes at 400° to sear meat and hold in juices. Lower oven to 300° and cook approximately 25 minutes per pound. Insert meat thermometer in center of roast, through top layer of fat. Roast will register 140° for rare, 160° for medium, 170° for well done. Remember, the outer slices will be a bit more well done than the center.

When meat is done, remove meat thermometer and transfer to serving plate. Let rest about 10 minutes before carving to let roast absorb its juices and become easier to carve.

After the roast is removed, pour a little cold water into pan to dissolve the drippings. Defat drippings, reheat and serve "au jus" with meat. Very little juice will have escaped from the meat and drippings will be mostly fat so amount of "au jus" will be small. If desired, you may want to extend "au jus" with consomme, bouillon or beef stock.

Accompany with horseradish sauce.

Holiday perfect with stuffed potatoes.

LONDON BROIL

Serves 2

1 Serving = 165 Calories

3 Low Fat Meat Exchanges

8 ounces flank steak

Salt and pepper

Garlic powder

Cut flank steak in strips, divide in half, roll (jelly roll style) and skewer. Broil 3 inches from heat turning once to attain desired doneness. Season with garlic, salt and pepper.

BROILED BEEF STEAKS

1 Serving (4 ounces) = 225 Calories
3 Med Fat Meat Exchanges

Beef Steaks (porterhouse, T-bone, sirloin, rib,
New York, or tenderloin)

Allow about 4 ounces meat per person without bone and fat. Set oven to broil and place meat 2 inches from heat. Broil about 5 minutes on each side for rare meat, about 7 minutes for medium or 8-9 minutes for well done.

When steaks are browned on one side sprinkle with salt, pepper and a bit of garlic powder if desired. Turn and broil second side. Test for doneness by cutting a small slit in meat. On bone-in pieces cut next to bone to test for doneness. When ready, season second side and serve immediately.

BEEF KEBOB

Serves 6
1 Serving = 135 Calories
2 Low Fat Meat Exchanges
1 Vegetable Exchange

1 pound lean beef cubes
1 chopped green pepper
12 small boiling onions
12 cherry tomatoes
12 mushrooms
½ recipe for teriyaki sauce

Wash beef and marinate in teriyaki sauce for 4-6 hours or overnight. Wash and clean out center of green pepper and cut into 1 inch pieces. Peel onions and parboil 3-4 minutes.

Arrange cubes of beef on skewers alternating with the tomatoes, mushrooms, green pepper and onions. Oven broil or charcoal barbecue until desired doneness. Baste occasionally while cooking. Turn to cook evenly. Careful—skewers get hot!

BEEF STEW

Serves 4
1 Serving = 265 Calories
3 Low Fat Meat Exchanges
1 Bread Exchange
1 Vegetable Exchange

1 pound boneless lean beef cubes
4 small potatoes
3 carrots
1 medium onion
Salt and pepper

Brown beef cubes in salt over medium heat. Add enough warm water to cover and simmer in covered pan one to one and half hours. Wash, peel and cut vegetables in quarters. Place in pan adding a bit more water if needed. Cover and simmer one more hour until vegetables are tender. Season to taste. Delicious served with dumplings. (Remember to add the dumpling calories and exchange.)

*I often buy round steak or the end off a large boneless roast and cut into cubes for nice lean economical stew meat.

SWISS STEAK

Serves 4
1 Serving = 210 Calories
2 Med Fat Meat Exchanges
½ Bread Exchange
½ Fat Exchange

12 ounces tenderized round steak
1 can onion soup in beef broth
½ soup can water
Salt

Cut meat into four servings and trim off fat. Brown meat in hot skillet in salt. Pour soup over meat and add half can of warm water to pan. Lift meat to allow liquid to flow underneath. Cover and simmer on top of the stove 1½ to 2 hours until tender or bake in 325° oven 1½ - 2 hours.

*If desired you may thicken juices after removing meat. Mix 1 tablespoon cornstarch in 2 tablespoons cold water. Stir over medium heat until thickened. Serve with meat.

CORNED BEEF & CABBAGE

NEW ENGLAND BOILED DINNER
(One Pot Meal)

Serves 6
1 Serving = 420 Calories
4 Med Fat Meat Exchanges
2 Vegetable Exchanges
1 Bread Exchange

1 (3 pound) corned beef round
6 small potatoes, pared
6 small carrots, pared
6 wedges cabbage (1 head)

Place corned beef in covered pot with hot water to cover. Bring to boil and simmer 2 hours. Add carrots and potatoes and continue simmering an additional hour. Add cabbage and cook 20 minutes longer.

Remove meat and vegetables and drain a minute before serving. Carve meat in thin slices across the grain.

Corned beef will shrink, but is excellent leftover cold for sandwiches.

SAUCY PORK CHOPS

4 Servings
1 Serving = 305 Calories
3 Med Fat Meat Exchanges
½ Bread Exchange
1 Fat Exchange

4 (4 ounce) loin pork chops, fat removed
1 can Cream of Chicken soup
3 tablespoons catsup
½ teaspoon onion powder
2 tablespoons Worchestershire sauce

Brown pork chops in salt over medium heat. Combine soup, catsup, Worchestershire sauce and onion. Pour over chops. Bake at 350° for 40 minutes covered; uncover and bake an additional ten minutes. Serve in sauce.

BAKED HAM SLICE

Serves 4
1 Serving = 185 Calories
3 Low Fat Meat Exchanges
½ Fruit Exchange

1 ham slice (1 pound about ¾ to 1 inch thick)
1 pinch ground cloves
¼ teaspoon dry mustard
½ cup unsweetened pineapple juice
2 slices unsweetened pineapple
2 tablespoons water
Paprika

Blend dry mustard with pineapple juice and cloves. Pour over ham slice. Top with pineapple rings. Bake at 350° for 25-30 minutes. Sprinkle lightly with paprika.

COMPANY BAKED HAM

1 Slice (2 × 3 × ⅛) = 55 Calories
1 Low Fat Meat Exchange

Ham, smoked ready to eat
Unsweetened pineapple rings, as garnish
10 whole cloves (6 per pound)

Bake at 350° for 10 minutes per pound. Remove rind, if any, and garnish with cloves and pineapple rings the last 20 minutes of cooking time. Secure pineapple with toothpicks. If pineapple is eaten count in daily fruit allowance.

QUICK VEAL SCALLOPINE

Serves 4
1 Serving = 235 Calories
3 Low Fat Meat Exchanges
1 Vegetable Exchange
1 Fat Exchange

1 pound veal (cut or pounded thin)
4 teaspoons margarine
¼ cup diet ginger ale
1 tablespoon lemon juice
1 clove crushed garlic
¼ teaspoon oregano
Salt and pepper
1 cup mushrooms

Brown veal in margarine. Add the liquid, garlic, oregano, salt and pepper. Simmer 10 minutes. Add mushrooms and simmer an additional 5-10 minutes. Garnish with lemon. Serve with rice or noodles.

VEAL OR BEEF BIRDS

Serves 6
1 Serving = 325 Calories
3 Low Fat Meat Exchanges
1 Bread Exchange
2 Fat Exchanges

1½ pounds tenderized veal or beef round
1½ cups stuffing
Salt
1 can Cream of Mushroom soup
¾ soup can water to dilute soup
1 tablespoon sherry (optional)

Cut meat into six equal pieces. Spread stuffing on each piece. Roll and secure with toothpicks. Brown meat in salt. Add diluted soup and sherry over meat rolls. Bake in 325° oven about 40 minutes.

SIMPLE VEAL CASSEROLE

Serves 4
1 Serving = 225 Calories
3 Low Fat Meat Exchanges
¼ Bread Exchange
1 Fat Exchange

1 pound boneless veal
1 can Cream of Mushroom soup
½ soup can dry white wine

Brown meat in salt. Add soup that has been diluted with wine. Bake covered in 350° oven for 45-50 minutes.

BROILED LAMB CHOPS

Serves 4
1 Serving = 165 Calories
3 Low Fat Meat Exchanges

4 chops (rib or loin)
    approximately 5 ounces with bone and 4 ounces boneless
Salt and pepper
Garlic powder

    Trim back fat and remove heavy layer to protect delicate flavor of meat. Broil 3 inches from heat about 8 minutes. Turn, season with salt, pepper and garlic powder to taste and continue broiling 5-8 minutes until done. Do not overcook as lamb will dry out and flavor will be lost.

MARINATED LAMB CHOPS

Serves 4-6
1 Serving = 165 Calories
3 Low Fat Meat Exchanges

4-6 (4 ounce) lamb chops
½ cup soy sauce
½ cup water
1 clove garlic, chopped
⅛ teaspoon pepper

Trim back outside fat, combine all ingredients and refrigerate covered overnight. Broil or barbecue about 8 minutes; turn and continue cooking about 5 minutes or until desired doneness.

SEAFOOD STUFFED TOMATO

2 Servings
1 Serving = 180 Calories
2 Low Fat Meat Exchanges
1 Vegetable Exchange
1 Fat Exchange

2 ounces crab
2 ounces shrimp
1 rib chopped celery
½ teaspoon chopped onion
2 teaspoons mayonnaise
2 tomatoes
½ teaspoon lemon juice
Salt and pepper to taste

Peel tomatoes, cut off top and scoop out center. Drain upside down while mixing remaining ingredients. Fill tomato with seafood mixture. Serve chilled on a bed of lettuce. Garnish with lemon wedge.

If desired, use all shrimp or all crabmeat.

SALADS, DRESSINGS
and
VEGETABLES

TUNA SALAD

6 Servings
1 Serving = 155 Calories
2 Low Fat Meat Exchanges
1 Fat Exchange

½ cup low calorie mayonnaise
1 tablespoon lemon juice
2 tablespoons chopped green onions (tops and all)
¼ teaspoon salt
2 (6½ ounces) cans water-packed tuna
½ cup chopped celery

Combine all ingredients and toss slightly before serving. Serve on a bed of shredded lettuce.

TUNA STUFFED TOMATO

1 Serving = 180 Calories
2 Low Fat Meat Exchanges
1 Fat Exchange
1 Vegetable Exchange

1 serving tuna salad recipe (preceding recipe)
1 large tomato

Wash and carefully cut tomato in wedges leaving one end connected. Open tomato like a flower and fill with tuna salad. Garnish with parsley sprig or lemon wedge if desired.
Serve on bed of lettuce leaves.

SHRIMP-CABBAGE SALAD

4 Servings
1 Serving = 125 Calories
1 Low Fat Meat Exchange
1 Fat Exchange
1 Vegetable Exchange

½ head finely shredded cabbage
4 ounces salad shrimp
2 teaspoons lemon juice
¼ cup low calorie mayonnaise
Salt and pepper to taste

If I use this for a main lunch entree I double the shrimp. Add one low fat meat exchange and 55 calories.

SEAFOOD SALAD

Serves 6
1 Serving = 235 Calories
3 Low Fat Meat Exchanges
1 Fat Exchange
1 Vegetable Exchange

1 pound crab, shrimp, salmon or a combination
1 cup chopped celery
2 tablespoons chopped dill pickles
1 tablespoon chopped onion
2 hard-boiled eggs, chopped
½ teaspoon salt
¼ teaspoon pepper
⅓ cup mayonnaise
2 tomatoes cut in six pieces
1 small head chopped lettuce

Drain any canned seafood. Combine all ingredients except lettuce and tomatoes. Serve on lettuce bed and garnish with two tomato wedges.

SUMMER SALAD

10-12 Servings
½ Cup Serving = 25 Calories
1 Vegetable Exchange

Layer in glass bowl in order given.

4 chunked tomatoes with skins
2 chopped sweet onions
4 salad cucumbers, pared and sliced
4 sprigs chopped fresh parsley

Marinate at least 2 hours in Good Seasons Low Calorie Italian Dressing, prepared as package directs. Serve with slotted spoon.

V-8 VEGETABLE MOLD

4-5 Servings
½ Cup Serving = 25 Calories
1 Vegetable Exchange

1½ cups V-8 juice
1 envelope gelatin
1 tablespoon lemon juice
¼ cup diced celery
¼ cup diced green onion (tops too)
¼ cup diced green pepper
¼ cup diced cucumber

In a saucepan over medium heat combine V-8 juice and gelatin. Stir until gelatin is dissolved. Add lemon juice and vegetables. Chill until firm. Attractive when served on a bed of lettuce.

CRANBERRY-APPLE MOLD

8 Servings
1 Serving = 12 Calories
¼ Fruit Exchange

2 cups low calorie cranberry juice cocktail
1 (4 serving) envelope low calorie orange gelatin
1 cup chopped apple
½ cup chopped celery

Bring 1 cup of juice to boil and stir in gelatin until dissolved. Add remaining juice. Chill until thickened. Stir in apple (with the peel on) and celery.

Pour in one quart (4 cup) mold. Pretty served on bed of lettuce.

MARINATED CUCUMBERS AND ONIONS

8 Servings
1 Serving = 40 Calories
¼ Low Fat Meat Exchange
1 Vegetable Exchange

Mix Together:
1 cup mock sour cream
2 tablespoons wine vinegar
Artificial sweetener to equal 4 teaspoons sugar
½ teaspoon salt
¼ teaspoon pepper
1 tablespoon chopped chives, fresh or frozen
1 tablespoon dill seed

Add: 2 thinly sliced salad onions
2 thinly sliced cucumbers

Refrigerate before serving and sprinkle lightly with paprika.

DILL PICKLES

Free Food

Brine - 1 quart cider vinegar
      3 quarts cold water
      1 cup pickling salt

Bring brine to boil and pour over packed quart jars; seal immediately. Let age 2 months.

Pack into hot sterilized jars:

1 large clove garlic
2 heads dill
1 small red pepper (optional)
Small cucumbers

Continue as directed above.

*Hard water makes soft pickles; soft water makes crispy pickles.
These pickles were blue ribbon winners at the fair.

PICKLED BEETS

Serves 4
½ Cup = 25 Calories
1 Vegetable Exchange

¼ cup water
⅓ cup vinegar
Artificial sweetener to equal ½ cup sugar
¼ teaspoon salt
¼ teaspoon ground cloves
1 can (about 2 cups) diced or sliced beets

Bring all ingredients but beets to a boil. Add beets and simmer 5 minutes. Chill. Serve cold as a vegetable or relish. I like them mixed in a green salad.

DILLED ONIONS
(Self-Pickling)

½ Cup = 25 Calories
1 Vegetable Exchange

Cut onions in ¼ inch slices. Cover with leftover dill pickle juice. Refrigerate covered at least three days to absorb flavor.

Good on sandwiches, as a relish or a new flavor in salad. Juice may be used several times.

I often put leftover cooked green beans or cauliflower and broccoli in the pickle juice for salad use.

MUSHROOMS IN WINE

Serves 2
1 Serving = 75 Calories
1 Vegetable Exchange
1 Fat Exchange

½ pound mushrooms
2 teaspoons butter
½ teaspoon Lawry's Seasoned Salt
¼ teaspoon garlic powder
2 tablespoons dry wine

Clean and slice mushrooms. Melt butter in frying pan. Add mushrooms and seasonings. Saute until tender. Add wine and simmer 2-3 minutes for flavors to develop. Serve hot with steak or roast.

SAUTEED MUSHROOMS

Serves 2
1 Serving = 70 Calories
1 Vegetable Exchange
1 Fat Exchange

½ pound mushrooms
2 teaspoons butter
Dash salt and pepper
Seasoning salt or garlic salt to taste

Clean and slice large mushrooms (small ones may be kept whole). Melt butter in small frying pan. Add mushrooms and seasonings; saute about three minutes until tender but not limp. Delicious with broiled steak.

BROCCOLI WITH LEMON SAUCE

Serves 4
1 Serving = 25 Calories
1 Vegetable Exchange

1 large bunch broccoli
1 tablespoon lemon juice
1 tablespoon water or sugar free lemon-lime soda
Artificial sweetener to equal 1 teaspoon sugar (if desired)

Clean and trim broccoli. Cut stalks and flowerettes into about 3 inch "trees." Simmer gently about 12 minutes covered with water. Drain. Mix lemon juice, liquid, and sweetener. Trickle over broccoli. I like to heat the lemon mixture to help keep the vegetable warm.

The lemon sauce is good on any green vegetable.

BROILED TOMATO HALVES

Serves 2
1 Serving = 50 Calories
1 Vegetable Exchange
½ Fat Exchange

1 large tomato
2 teaspoons grated parmesan cheese
1 teaspoon oregano
1 teaspoon butter or margarine
2 teaspoons dried bread crumbs

Cut tomato in half crosswise. Place on broiling pan. Combine remaining ingredients and top each tomato half with ½ of mixture. Broil 3 inches from the heat until tomatoes are warm and topping lightly brown. Broiling keeps tomatoes firm but makes them tender.

Leave the skin on the tomatoes or they will turn to mush.

SPICY TOMATO DRESSING

Free Food

1 cup tomato juice
¾ teaspoon unflavored gelatin
1½ teaspoons dry salad dressing mix of your choice
1 tablespoon wine vinegar

Bring ½ cup tomato juice to boil and add gelatin. Stir until dissolved. Add remaining ingredients, blend thoroughly. Chill. Shake before serving.
(Gelatin makes the dressing thick.)

FREE SALAD DRESSING

Free Food

½ cup tomato juice
2 tablespoons lemon juice
½ teaspoon horseradish
1 tablespoon finely chopped onion
Salt and pepper

Combine ingredients. Refrigerate. Shake well before serving.

CALORIE WATCHERS' DRESSING

Free Food
Makes ½ cup

4 tablespoons wine vinegar
2 tablespoons water
Sugar substitute to equal 1 teaspoon sugar
¼ teaspoon salt
¼ teaspoon paprika
1 clove crushed garlic

Put all ingredients into blender and whip until well blended.

COLE SLAW DRESSING

16 Servings
1 Tablespoon = 25 Calories
½ Fat Exchange
If more than 1 tablespoon
    is used, meat exchange
    must be considered

½ cup mock sour cream
½ cup mayonnaise
1 teaspoon grated onion
2 tablespoons lemon juice
Artificial sweetener to equal 2 tablespoons sugar
¼ teaspoon pepper
1 teaspoon celery seed

Blend ingredients together and use over cabbage that has been sliced thin or coarsely chopped.

CARROT-RAISIN SALAD

2 Servings
1 Serving = 90 Calories
½ Fruit Exchange
1 Vegetable Exchange
1 Fat Exchange

2 tablespoons raisins
1 cup boiling water
1 cup shredded carrots
1 tablespoon lemon juice
2 teaspoons mayonnaise

Soak raisins in boiling water ½ hour. Drain well. Mix all ingredients and chill.

CHEESY PEAR SALAD

1 Serving = 65 Calories
½ Fruit Exchange
1 Fat Exchange

½ fresh or canned pear without sugar
1 tablespoon cream cheese topping
Lettuce leaf

Place pear half on lettuce leaf. Top with cream cheese topping.

FRUIT AND COTTAGE CHEESE SALAD

Serves 1
1 Serving = 95 Calories
1 Med Fat Meat Exchange
½ Fruit Exchange

¼ cup cottage cheese
½ peach, pear or slice of pineapple (fresh or canned
    without sugar)
Lettuce leaf

Arrange fruit on lettuce leaf cut side up. Top with cottage cheese. Serve cold.

FRUIT CUP

½ Cup = 40 Calories
1 Fruit Exchange

Fresh fruit is colorful, tasty and refreshing, and a mixture in a bright dish is a welcome change of pace.

One-half cup of any combination of the following equals 1 fruit exchange: apples, oranges, berries, grapefruit, nectarines, peaches, pears, pineapple or tangerines.

MOCK RICE PILAF

1 Serving
½ Cup = 70 Calories
1 Bread Exchange

Use chicken or beef bouillon in the place of water to cook rice.
Tasty and a real complement to the main course.

SPANISH RICE

4 Servings
1 Serving = 85 Calories
1 Bread Exchange
½ Vegetable Exchange

2 cups cooked rice
2 teaspoons diced green pepper
½ chopped onion
2 teaspoons pimento bits
1 teaspoon salt
½ teaspoon pepper
1 cup tomato juice
1 teaspoon Worchestershire sauce

Mix all ingredients together and bake at 350° for 30 minutes or until heated through and bubbly. Fluff with fork before serving.

STUFFED POTATOES

4 Servings
1 Serving = 100 Calories
1 Bread Exchange
¼ High Fat Meat Exchange
Milk Negligible

2 large baked potatoes
2 tablespoons skim milk
½ teaspoon onion powder
¼ cup grated cheddar cheese
Salt and pepper to taste
Paprika for garnish

Cut baked potatoes in half lengthwise. Carefully scoop out centers leaving shells intact. Mash centers with milk, onion powder, and salt and pepper. Stir in grated cheese. Sprinkle tops with paprika. Reheat in 400° oven until warm through. Great to do ahead for busy days or company meals.

RAW FRIES

Serves 2
1 Serving = 115 Calories
1 Fat Exchange
1 Bread Exchange

2 teaspoons bacon fat
2 small potatoes, peeled
1 tablespoon chopped onion (optional)
1 tablespoon water

Heat fat over medium heat in frying pan. Cube potatoes and add to fat. Add onion if desired. Add water and cover 5 minutes. Remove cover and cook until brown on the bottom. With spatula turn over and brown on the other side. Salt and pepper as desired.

POTATO SALAD

Serves 6
1 Serving = 190 Calories
1 Bread Exchange
½ Med Fat Meat Exchange
2 Fat Exchanges

2 large potatoes (boiled, peeled, cubed)
3 hard-boiled eggs, chopped
¼ cup mayonnaise
½ teaspoon mustard
¼ cup chopped dill pickle
¼ cup chopped onion (or to taste)
½ cup chopped celery
1 teaspoon salt
½ teaspoon pepper
Chopped pimento (optional)

Mix ingredients and chill. If more moisture is desired, add a small amount of dill pickle juice.

OVEN-BROWNED POTATOES

4 Servings
1 Serving = 70 Calories
1 Bread Exchange

4 small potatoes
2 tablespoons defatted drippings

Boil peeled potatoes until almost done, drain. Coat with defatted drippings and leave remaining drippings in pan. Bake in 325° oven for 20-30 minutes. Turn to brown evenly. Season with salt and pepper if desired.

*I often remove and defat roast drippings an hour before a roast is done and then oven brown potatoes the last 30 minutes the roast is in the oven.

BAKED POTATOES

1 Small Potato = 70 Calories
1 Bread Exchange

Scrub potatoes well. Bake at 400° for one hour or until soft to pressure. To fluff up, knead gently in a towel, cut top criss-cross and press ends.

To keep the potato low calorie and save your fat exchanges, try one of the topping recipes.

For light fluffy baked potatoes, do not wrap in foil, as they steam in foil, not bake.

BAKED POTATO NUGGETS

Serves 4
1 Serving = 48 Calories
½ Bread Exchange
¼ Fat Exchange

2 medium potatoes
1 teaspoon butter or margarine
Salt and pepper

Scrub potatoes and cut in half lengthwise. Rub each potato with butter and sprinkle with salt and pepper. Bake at 375° for 45 minutes. Will be fork tender inside and crispy skinned.

OVEN FRENCH FRIES

Serves 3
1 Serving = 115 Calories
1 Bread Exchange
1 Fat Exchange

3 small potatoes, peeled
1 tablespoon butter or margarine
Salt

Cut raw potatoes lengthwise. Place ½ butter in small flat pan. Arrange potato pieces on butter. Melt the other half of the butter and brush on potatoes. Bake at 375° until tender. Turn often to brown and crisp on all sides. Salt and serve.

PLAIN SCALLOPED POTATOES

Serves 4
1 Serving = 90 Calories
¼ Milk Exchange
1 Bread Exchange

2 cups peeled sliced potatoes (4 small)
Salt and pepper
1 cup skim milk

Layer potatoes in casserole, seasoning layers as you fill dish. Pour milk over potatoes and bake in 350° oven for approximately 45 minutes.

SEASONED SCALLOPED POTATOES

Serves 4
1 Serving = 97 Calories
1 Bread Exchange
¼ Vegetable Exchange
¼ Milk Exchange

2 cups potatoes (4 small or 2 large)
1 large onion
Salt and pepper
1 cup skim milk

Alternate layers of peeled sliced potatoes and thinly sliced onions. Season and pour milk over all. Bake in 350° oven for approximately 45 minutes.

SKINNY SCALLOPED POTATOES

8 Servings
1 Serving = 70 Calories
1 Bread Exchange

4 cups peeled sliced potatoes
1 can sliced mushrooms, drained (optional)
¼ cup sliced green onions (tops too)
½ teaspoon salt
¼ teaspoon pepper
¼ teaspoon thyme
4 bouillon cubes
1½ cups boiling water

Layer potatoes, mushrooms, and green onions in 1½ quart baking dish. Dissolve bouillon cubes in boiling water, and add seasoning. Pour over vegetable mixture. Bake covered for 45 minutes at 350°. Remove cover and continue cooking an additional 15-20 minutes.

*I use beef bouillon with red meat dishes and chicken with poultry and white meat dishes.

LEMON CARROTS

Serves 6
½ Cup = 70 Calories
1 Vegetable Exchange
1 Fat Exchange

3 cups sliced carrots
¾ cup water
½ teaspoon salt
½ teaspoon freshly grated lemon peel
2 teaspoons fresh lemon juice
1 tablespoon fresh chopped parsley
2 tablespoons butter
Dash of liquid sweetener (to taste)

Wash and peel carrots and slice in ¼ inch rounds. Bring water to boil in saucepan, add carrots and salt. Cook until tender (10-15 minutes) covered. Drain. In saucepan add remaining ingredients until butter is melted. Toss like a salad to coat all carrots. Serve hot.

SWEETS

BAKED CUSTARD

3 Servings
1 Serving = 80 Calories
½ Whole Milk Exchange

1 egg
1 cup milk
Artificial sweetener to equal 1 tablespoon sugar
1 teaspoon vanilla
Nutmeg
¼ teaspoon salt

Break egg into small mixing bowl and beat slightly. Add remaining ingredients and beat well. Pour into damp (run under water, remove excess, leaving slight film) custard cups and sprinkle well with nutmeg. Bake in 350° oven in a shallow pan of water 40-50 minutes. A silver knife inserted in the center will come out clean when custard is done.

COCONUT CUSTARD

12 Servings
1 Serving = 80 Calories
¼ Skim Milk Exchange
½ Med Fat Meat Exchange
½ Fat Exchange

2¾ cup scalded skim milk
6 eggs
Artificial sweetener to equal ½ cup sugar
¼ teaspoon salt
1 teaspoon vanilla
¾ cup unsweetened coconut
Nutmeg as desired

Combine eggs, sweetener, salt, and vanilla in a large mixing bowl and blend well. Slowly add the scalded milk and beat slightly. Mix coconut in gently. Pour into a lightly buttered 8-inch square baking dish and sprinkle top with nutmeg. Bake 5 minutes at 450° and reduce heat to 350° for an additional 15 minutes. Silver knife inserted in center will come out clean when done.

This custard would be good in a pie shell.

LEMON FILLING

Per Recipe = 75 Calories
1 Med Fat Meat Exchange

This fills an individual tart shell. Recipe can be doubled, tripled, etc., to accommodate whatever type pie shell you are filling. It also is good just as a pudding.

1 teaspoon (⅓ envelope) gelatin (unflavored)
2 tablespoons lemon juice
1 egg yolk
1 teaspoon lemon peel
½ cup diet lemon soda
Artificial sweetener to equal 6 teaspoons sugar

Soften gelatin in lemon juice. Combine remaining ingredients with wire whip. Blend well and stir over low heat (to avoid sticking), until mixture thickens. Pour into tart or pie shell.

CREAM PIE FILLING

Use packaged sugar free pudding mixes as directed. Pour into graham cracker or baked pastry shell. Refrigerate.

For an additional treat, line pie shell with fresh fruit (bananas, peaches, etc.) before adding pudding. Be sure to add in fruit exchanges.

MERINGUE

Free Food
Exchanges Negligible

3 egg whites
⅜ teaspoons cream of tartar
Artificial sweetener equal to 1 tablespoon sugar (I use granulated type)

Beat egg whites with cream of tartar until stiff. Add sweetener while still beating on high speed. Top pie or pudding. Bake in 400° oven about 8 minutes until lightly browned and set.

BERRY PIE

Serves 6
1 Serving = 245 Calories
1 Fruit Exchange
1 Bread Exchange
3 Fat Exchanges

3 cups Black or Boysen berries
¼ teaspoon cinnamon
2 tablespoons tapioca
Artificial sweetener to equal ¾ cup sugar
1 unbaked pastry crust recipe, divided to make top and bottom crust in 8-inch pan

Mix fruit, cinnamon, tapioca and sweetener. Put into unbaked pie shell. Top with other crust. Cut slits in top crust for steam to escape. Bake at 425° about 40 minutes.

APPLE PIE

8 Servings
1 Serving = 200 Calories
1 Fruit Exchange
1 Bread Exchange
2 Fat Exchanges

1 unbaked pastry recipe, divided and rolled thin
   (½ for bottom crust, ½ for top)
4 cups sliced apples
Artificial sweetener to equal 1 cup
1 tablespoon lemon juice
½ - 1 teaspoon cinnamon or nutmeg
1 teaspoon flour

     Mix apples, sweetener, lemon juice, spice and flour. Pour into pastry lined pie pan (8 or 9 inches) and top with other crust. Cut slits in top crust to vent steam. Bake at 425° for 40-45 minutes. Serve warm or cold.

GRAHAM CRACKER CRUST

Serves 6
1 Serving = 115 Calories
1 Bread Exchange
1 Fat Exchange

12 graham crackers (squares)
2 tablespoons melted butter
Artificial sugar equal to 2 tablespoons sugar

Crush graham crackers. Melt butter and mix with crackers and sweetener. Press into 8 inch pie pan. Refrigerate 1 hour before filling.

PASTRY CRUST

8 Servings
1 Serving = 150 Calories
1 Bread Exchange
2 Fat Exchanges

1 cup flour
Dash of salt
⅓ cup shortening
2 tablespoons cold water

Mix flour and salt in bowl. Add shortening and cut into flour until about the size of peas. Add water and mix into a ball. Roll out on lightly floured pastry canvas. Makes enough crust for one 9-10 inch shell or 8-inch two crust pie if pastry is rolled thin.

To bake empty shell prick entire crust with fork (to prevent bubbles) and bake 7-9 minutes at 425° until a delicate golden brown. Fill when cool.

CREAM PUFF/ECLAIR SHELLS

Makes 6
1 Puff = 135 Calories
½ Bread Exchange
½ Med Fat Meat Exchange
1½ Fat Exchanges

½ cup water
¼ cup butter
½ cup flour
2 eggs

Heat water and butter to rolling boil in saucepan. Stir in flour and keep stirring until mixture forms a ball. Remove from heat and beat in eggs one at a time. Beat until smooth. Drop from spoon on ungreased cookie sheet. Bake at 400° approximately 40 minutes. Shells should be puffed, dry and golden brown.

Cool away from drafts, cut off tops and remove soft centers. Fill as desired.

REAL STRAWBERRY SHORTCAKE

Per Person = 155 Calories
1 Bread Exchange
1 Fruit Exchange
1 Fat Exchange

1 cup strawberries
1 baking powder biscuit, 2-inch diameter
1 tablespoon whipping cream
1 drop vanilla
Artificial sweetener

Wash and slice or mash the berries (leave one whole for the top). Split the biscuit and spoon half the berries in the center; replace the top and add the remaining berries. Whip the cream and sweeten to taste. Add drop of vanilla to cream and top shortcake. Garnish with whole ripe berry.

POPSICLES/FLAVORED ICE CUBES

Free Exchange

Simply freeze diet soda in ice trays and add sticks. To stop the "drippys" I often heat soda with 1 tablespoon gelatin before freezing.

I often use these ice cubes for color or as a "flavor saver" in cold beverages.

DESSERT TOPPING

Makes 1 Cup
1 Tablespoon = 15 Calories
¼ Med Fat Meat Exchange
Milk Negligible

3 tablespoons skim milk
1 cup cottage cheese
½ teaspoon vanilla
Sugar substitute equal to 1 tablespoon sugar

Put all ingredients into blender and whip until smooth. Makes a dessert out of fresh fruit.

TANGERINE-ORANGE SHERBET

Approximately 22 Servings
½ Cup = 60 Calories
¼ Skim Milk Exchange
1 Fruit Exchange

1 (6 ounce) can unsweetened frozen orange juice concentrate
1 (6 ounce) can unsweetened frozen tangerine juice concentrate
3½ cups cold water
1 cup non-fat dry milk solids
Artificial sweetener to equal 1 cup sugar

Pour all ingredients into 2 quart bowl in order. Beat just enough to blend. Freeze until slushy—about half frozen. Remove from the freezer and beat on low speed until softened, then on highest speed until light and creamy but not liquid. Pour into freezer containers and freeze.

The sherbet also is good all orange.

CANNED FRUIT COBBLER
(Cherries, Peaches, Blackberries)

Serves 4
1 Serving = 155 Calories
1 Fruit Exchange
1 Bread Exchange
1 Fat Exchange

1 can (No. 303) water-packed fruit
1 tablespoon cornstarch
⅔ cup fruit juice (drained off can)
½ teaspoon lemon juice
⅛ teaspoon almond extract
¼-½ teaspoon cinnamon (to taste)
¼ teaspoon liquid artificial sweetener
½ cup flour
½ teaspoon baking powder
⅛ teaspoon salt
1 egg
1 tablespoon butter or margarine
Artificial sugar to equal ½ cup sugar

Place canned fruit in baking pan. (It is easy to divide up in a small pie pan.) Mix cornstarch, drained fruit juice, lemon juice, sweetener, almond and cinnamon in small saucepan and cook until clear and thickened. Pour over fruit.

Mix together dry ingredients. Add slightly beaten egg, butter and sweetener and heat until well blended. Drop mounds of dough (2 tablespoons each) on top of fruits and bake in hot oven (425°) for 15 minutes.

Good warm with or without whipped topping.

WHIPPED TOPPING

Makes 1 Cup
$\frac{1}{4}$ Cup = 25 Calories
$\frac{1}{4}$ Skim Milk Exchange

$\frac{1}{4}$ cup non-fat dry milk solids
$\frac{1}{4}$ cup ice water
Artificial sweetener to equal 1 tablespoon sugar

Combine ingredients and beat on high speed of mixer until consistency of whipped cream. More sugar substitute may be added if a sweeter topping is desired.

APPLE COBBLER

Serves 8
1 Serving = 98 Calories
1 Fruit Exchange
½ Bread Exchange
½ Fat Exchange

8 small apples, peeled and sliced
Artificial sweetener to equal ¾ cup sugar
½ teaspoon cinnamon
2 tablespoons flour
1 tablespoon lemon juice
1 teaspoon vanilla
½ teaspoon salt
¼ cup water

Mix above ingredients in 8 × 8 × 2 pan. In small bowl mix the following:

½ cup flour
Artificial sweetener to equal ½ cup sugar
½ teaspoon baking powder
¼ teaspoon salt
2 tablespoons soft butter
1 egg

Drop in eight equal mounds atop apple mixture. Bake at 375° for 35-40 minutes
Cut in 2 inch squares. Serve warm.

LEMON FROSTING

Serves 4
1 Serving = 65 Calories
¼ Milk Exchange
1 Fat Exchange

4 teaspoons butter
1 tablespoon lemon juice
⅓ cup non-fat dry milk
Artificial sweetener to equal 1 tablespoon sugar for tart icing, more if desired.

Melt butter. Add juice, dry milk powder and sweetener. Mix thoroughly and spread.

CHOCOLATE FROSTING

4 Servings
1 Serving = 65 Calories
1 Fat Exchange
¼ Milk Exchange

4 teaspoons butter
1 teaspoon chocolate extract
¼ teaspoon lemon juice
⅓ cup non-fat dry milk
Artificial sweetener to equal 1 tablespoon sugar or
    to taste

Melt butter. Add remaining ingredients and blend well. To drizzle icing or make thinner sauce-type frosting add a small amount of skim milk.

SPONGE CAKE

6 Servings
1 Serving = 75 Calories
½ Bread Exchange
½ Med Fat Meat Exchange

3 eggs
¼ cup cold water
Sugar substitute to equal ¾ cup sugar
¼ teaspoon vanilla
1 tablespoon lemon juice
¾ cup sifted flour
Dash salt
¼ teaspoon cream of tartar

Separate eggs. Beat egg yolks until thick and lemon colored. Add water, sweetener, vanilla and lemon juice to egg yolks, beat until thick and fluffy (about 8 minutes). Add flour and salt to egg mixture a little at a time on low speed or fold in gently by hand. Beat egg whites until foamy, add cream of tartar and beat until stiff. Fold batter into stiff egg whites. Bake in an ungreased 8 or 9 inch loaf pan at 325° approximately 1 hour.

BRAN-APPLESAUCE COOKIES

4 Dozen Cookies
2 Cookies = 80 Calories
¼ Fruit Exchange
½ Bread Exchange
¾ Fat Exchange

½ cup margarine or butter
Sugar substitute to equal ½ cup sugar
1 egg
1½ cups flour
½ teaspoon salt
1 teaspoon cinnamon
½ teaspoon nutmeg
½ teaspoon cloves
1 teaspoon baking soda
1 cup unsweetened applesauce
⅓ cup raisins
1 cup All-Bran

In mixing bowl mix butter, sweetener and egg until light and fluffy. Combine dry ingredients and add alternately with applesauce on low speed. Add raisins and bran and beat on low speed just until mixed. Drop by level tablespoonfuls on lightly greased cookie sheet, about 1 inch apart. Bake at 370° about 18 minutes or until golden brown.

OATMEAL FRUIT BAR COOKIES

24 Bars
2 Bars = 175 Calories
⅓ Fruit Exchange
1 Bread Exchange
2 Fat Exchanges

1 cup quick cooking rolled oats
1 cup flour
½ teaspoon salt
½ teaspoon cinnamon
1 teaspoon vanilla
Artificial sweetener to equal ½ cup sugar
½ cup shortening
2 cups drained water-packed canned fruit (save juice)
2 tablespoons reserved fruit juice

    Mix all ingredients except fruit and juice until mixture becomes coarse crumbs. Add the fruit juice to hold crumbs together. Press ½ of the crumbs into 8 × 8 inch square pan. Top with chopped or mashed fruit. Pat on remaining crumbs. Bake at 375° for 30 minutes. Cut into bars when cool.

RAISIN OATMEAL COOKIES

72 Cookies
1 Cookie = 30 Calories
¼ Bread Exchange
¼ Fat Exchange

1½ cups uncooked quick cooking oatmeal
⅔ cup melted butter
2 eggs
1 tablespoon liquid sweetener
1 teaspoon vanilla
1½ cups flour
½ teaspoon salt
2 teaspoons baking powder
¼ teaspoon cinnamon
⅛ teaspoon cloves
⅛ teaspoon nutmeg
⅛ teaspoon allspice
½ cup skim milk
½ cup raisins

Measure oatmeal into large mixing bowl. Stir in melted butter and mix well. Blend in eggs, sweetener and vanilla. Add dry ingredients alternately with milk. Add raisins. Drop by level teaspoonfuls on cookie sheet. Bake at 375° until golden brown, about 10 minutes.

QUICK CHOCOLATE BROWNIES

16 Big Brownies
1 Serving = 110 Calories
½ Bread Exchange
2 Fat Exchanges

¾ cup flour
1 cup dry sugar substitute
¼ cup cocoa
½ teaspoon salt
½ cup margarine
2 eggs
1 teaspoon vanilla
½ cup chopped nuts

Combine all ingredients in mixing bowl. Beat 3 minutes. Pour into lightly greased 8-inch square pan. Bake at 350° for 30 minutes. Cool, cut into squares.

There is no leavening agent...the eggs do it all!

SPICY COOKIES

24 Cookies
2 Cookies = 75 Calories
½ Bread Exchange
1 Fat Exchange

5 tablespoons butter
1 cup flour
¼ teaspoon baking powder
Artificial sweetener to equal ⅓ cup sugar
1 teaspoon cinnamon
2 teaspoons vanilla
1 tablespoon milk

Cream butter until light and fluffy. Blend in dry ingredients. Add vanilla and milk. Shape into little balls about ½ inch in diameter. Flatten with fork or three fingers to give a ridged effect. Bake at 375° about 12 minutes or until edges are brown.

WALNUT CRISPIES

24 Cookies
1 Cookie = 45 Calories
1 Fat Exchange

¼ cup butter
½ cup flour
½ cup chopped walnuts
½ teaspoon vanilla
¼ teaspoon salt
Artificial sweetener to equal 1 tablespoon sugar

Mix all ingredients and shape into small balls. Flatten out with bottom of a glass on ungreased cookie sheet. Bake at 300° about 45 minutes, or until light brown and crispy.

BAKED APPLES

Serves 6
1 Serving = 40 Calories
1 Fruit Exchange

6 small apples
Sugar substitute to equal ½ cup sugar
2 cups water
2 teaspoons vanilla
½ teaspoon cinnamon

Wash and core apples. Peel off collar around top. Place in baking dish. Put remaining ingredients in saucepan and bring to a boil. Pour over apples. Bake at 350° one hour. Apples will be soft but not mushy. Good warm or cold.

Garnish with whipped topping and cinnamon.

STEWED FRUIT

Serves 1 = 40 Calories
1 Fruit Exchange

1 fruit (fresh or dried)
¼ cup boiling water
Artificial sugar to equal 1 tablespoon sugar
Dash of cinnamon or cloves

    Peel and slice fresh fruit. Rinse dried fruit. Place in pan and cover with boiling water. Simmer until tender. Add sweetener and spice. Let stand 10 minutes. Refrigerate. Chill and serve.

GUM DROP CHEWS

Free Food

1 can fruit flavored diet soda
½ cup lemon juice
½ teaspoon vanilla
Artificial sweetener to equal ½ cup sugar
5 envelopes unflavored gelatin

Mix half can soda and all other ingredients in small mixing bowl.
Boil remaining soda and add to mixture, stirring until gelatin is dissolved.
Pour into 9 × 13 inch baking dish and refrigerate until firm. Cut into squares.

WORDS of WISDOM
and
INDEX

ARTIFICIAL SWEETENERS
Non-Caloric

Artificial sweeteners are available on the retail market in liquid, powder, tablets, cubes and granules. They replace sugar in sweetening power only and have no calories or food value.

Artificial sweetening agents do not provide the same bulk, texture or preservative quality of sugar. I most generally refrigerate artificially sweetened foods for safe-keeping.

When cooking with artificial sweeteners, be wary of their peculiarities. Undissolved powder or tablets will taste excessively sweet. To avoid this, simply crush and/or dissolve sweeteners in a bit of the liquid in a particular recipe, or mix in a small amount of water to use as desired.

Saccharin may give off a bitter flavor, especially after heating. To avoid this aftertaste, simply sweeten as near to the end of cooking as possible.

Products differ and experimenting will help you decide which textures, types and flavors you prefer. Equivalents are given on the labels and vary from product to product. Each time you buy a product check the label for changes in the sugar equivalent. As products are improved, the equivalent amounts often change.

I like the granulated forms for sprinkling on fruits and for most table use. The liquid in cold beverages is good and for cooking I usually evaluate the recipe and decide if a powder or liquid will blend best.

I often use diet lemon-lime soda for liquid as it adds a sweetener as well as moisture.

Too much artificial sweetener often leaves a bitter tang. Usually a little salt will counteract this objectionable taste.

HELPFUL HINTS

All foods in this book are measured according to the foods on the exchange lists using standard level household measuring cups and measuring spoons.

When purchasing meat, be fair to yourself: allow 4 ounces of lean raw meat for a 3 ounce portion and for poultry with skin and bones allow an extra 1½-2 ounces for skin and bones in a 4 ounce serving.

If adding extra fats in cooking, be sure you add the exchange and calories to your daily totals.

Brown meat on a hot skillet using salt to avoid sticking and save your fat exchange for something you really enjoy.

Be creative, add your own zest to meals by using your favorite herbs and spices in the recipes. Most herbs and spices are calorie free and may be used at will. If your family has a favorite, exchange it for the one I have used. (Example: some prefer sage stuffing, so exchange sage for poultry seasoning.) Caution—too many herbs and spices will mask your cooking effort. For a change of pace, I often add a bit of horseradish or chopped raw onions. A touch of this and that will add originality and variety to your cooking.

Use a bit of dry sugar-free fruit flavored gelatin to garnish whipped topping, fruits and puddings. It adds a bit of flavor and much color.

Taste-spoons of this and that while preparing meals are full of calories. Watch the extra bites to prevent the extra bulges.

INDEX BY RECIPE NAME

INDEX BY DIVIDED SECTIONS

SOUPS AND SANDWICHES

Clam Chowder, 56
Oyster Stew, 57
Quick Potato Soup, 55
Vegetable Soup, 54
Cheesy Dog, 63
Chicken Salad Sandwich, 64
Crab and Cheese Sandwich, 87

Grilled Crab and Cheese Sandwiches, 59
All-American Hamburger, 64
Hot Dog, 63
Mom's Special, 58
Open Face Sour Dough Crab Sandwiches, 60
Shrimp and Cheese, 87
Western Egg Sandwich, 41

SAUCES, TOPPINGS AND GRAVY

Blue Cheese Topping, 71
Cheese Sauce, 70
Cream Cheese Topping, 71
Free Gravy, 78
Ham Sauce, 76
Herb-Cheese Potato Topping, 73
Horseradish Sauce, 69
Jam, Fruit, 81
Jellied Cranberry Sauce, 75

Mock Sour Cream, 77
Mushroom Sauce, 77
Saucy Cheese Topping, 72
Seafood Cocktail Sauce, 66
Spaghetti Sauce, 82
Tartar Sauce, 67
Teriyaki Sauce, 68
Thin Maple Syrup, 80
White Sauce, 74

SALADS, DRESSINGS AND VEGETABLES

MAIN DISHES

SWEETS